One Page Management

One Page Management

How to Use Information to Achieve Your Goals

Riaz Khadem, Ph.D., and Robert Lorber, Ph.D.

WILLIAM MORROW AND COMPANY, INC.

New York

Library of Congress Cataloging-in-Publication Data

Khadem, Riaz.
One page management.

1. Management.   2. Organizational effectiveness.
I. Lorber, Robert.   II. Title.
HD38.K47   1986   658.4′038   85-82535
ISBN 0-688-06499-X

Printed in the United States of America

First Edition

1 2 3 4 5 6 7 8 9 10

Dedicated to those
men, women, and children
who are striving to establish
world peace

Introduction

This book describes the principles and techniques of One Page Management through the story of Brian Scott, newly appointed CEO of a troubled manufacturing company, Xcorp. As Scott begins his new assignment, he finds himself buried in a multitude of reports generated by the various departments of the company. Finding out what has been going on becomes a major challenge.

Xcorp could have been a financial institution, a hospital, or a hotel. The principles would be the same, and the story would be similar.

The ideas expressed in this book are the result of observing hundreds of managers at their places of work. These managers gave us a picture of the existing corporate cultures and helped us see the problems arising out of the way managers view their work, their performance, and the way they interact with information. They helped us develop the secrets of using information.

We hope that you will apply these secrets at work and at home, and that it will make a difference in your life and in the lives of those who work with you.

—RIAZ KHADEM
ROBERT LORBER

Foreword

In 1983, a year after the publication of *The One Minute Manager,* I asked Bob Lorber to join forces with me and write *Putting the One Minute Manager to Work.* I knew the three secrets of the One Minute Manager had been universally accepted as easy-to-understand and easy-to-apply management concepts, but I was worried about whether managers would really grab on to the philosophy and use it on a day-to-day basis in their organizations. I had been discouraged so many times by the fickle philosophy of most companies about management concepts. In fact one of my favorite sayings over the years has become MOST COMPANIES SPEND ALL THEIR TIME LOOKING FOR THE NEXT NEW MANAGEMENT CONCEPT AND LITTLE TIME FOLLOWING UP ON WHAT THEY JUST TAUGHT THEIR PEOPLE.

As a result, *Putting the One Minute Manager to Work* was all about implementing the three secrets—goal setting, praising, and reprimanding—in a systematic way. Bob's whole philosophy depends on organizations developing five effective systems:

1. Accountability System—Everyone has to be clear on what they are being asked to do.

2. Data System—Performance information must be gathered to determine how well people are doing.

3. Feedback System—Once the performance information has been gathered, feedback must be given to people so they can continue to perform well or redirect their efforts to get performance back on line.

4. Recognition System—Good performance must make a difference. So a recognition system based on performance is a must in high-performance organizations.

5. Training System—If people do not have the skills to perform well, they must be trained. High expectations without skills will only lead to frustration and poor performance.

Implementers from Lorber Kamai Associates, Inc., and Blanchard Training and Development, Inc., have done significant work in designing these systems in companies, but without the tools of a systematic information-gathering system. That's why Bob Lorber was excited when he met Riaz Khadem and learned about his One Page Management system. Riaz is an expert in the information business. His One Page Management approach adds "teeth" to the accountability, data, and feedback systems. Bob and I like to describe what Riaz does as turning a "high tech" information system into a "high touch" strategy—in John Naisbitt's term. In other words, he is able to take information and computer technology and make it available to managers so they can use information to "catch people doing things right," an important human factor.

With One Page Management, outstanding performance as well as recurring problems are communicated up the organizational ladder in such a way that MBWA (management by wandering around), made famous by Peters and Waterman's *In Search of Excellence,* can now become a more effective management tool. Just wandering around being nice to people has little impact. What really makes a difference is catching people doing things specifically right, and when problems recur, being ready to problem-solve.

My hat is off to Bob Lorber for seeing Riaz's information genius and encouraging him to translate his work in a way that can easily be understood by managers. I encouraged Riaz and Bob to use the One Minute Manager's powerful format in writing this book because it has proved to be the way managers like to learn. As a result, One Page Management is written as a parable in a clear, easy-to-understand way that should help everyone in all kinds of organizations use information in a way that creates a winning environment.

I recommend One Page Management without reservation. I think you'll find it helpful, and another step down the road to taking potentially complicated concepts and making them simple and usable to managers in every kind of organization.

—KENNETH H. BLANCHARD

Contents

PART I

*The
Information
Problem*

XCORP, a large U.S. conglomerate, was in trouble. The company had lost money over the previous six quarters. Sales were declining. Inventories were piling up and plants were shutting down. Xcorp's major competitors were growing strong.

The Xcorp Board of Directors met on a Friday morning and selected Brian Scott to be the new president and CEO. Scott had a successful track record. He had turned around two other companies in the past. One of these companies had gone from bankruptcy to profitability in just three years. Scott had a unique ability to get to the heart of the problem and implement effective solutions. He was dynamic, decisive, positive, and courageous. The Board was confident that Scott was the man they needed.

Scott bargained for two years of complete freedom to implement change. The Board accepted his condition. The challenge began.

It was a beautiful sunny Monday morning. Scott backed his car out of his garage and waved good-bye to his wife and two children. As he drove into the early morning traffic, he felt a thrill of excitement at the prospect of the day that lay before him.

He thought about the short-term strategy he had formulated to turn Xcorp around. It included drastic cost controls, reducing inventories, and paying careful attention to the company's cash position. It did not overrule the firing of some key people who were considered responsible for the current situation of the company.

Scott knew that he also needed a long-term solution to ensure the future growth of the company. The search for the long-term solution, however, was more difficult. As he rapidly approached the impressive Xcorp building to begin his first day as CEO, one idea kept coming to him.

*

*If
You Don't
Know
What's Wrong,*

*You
Can't Fix
It.*

*

Scott had studied Xcorp's financial statements. He knew that the company's profitability was dismal and worsening. Yet he was aware that the financial statements could not tell him the whole story. He suspected there were several factors to blame. To discover the real story behind the numbers, he decided to meet with the chief financial officer (CFO) of the corporation and get his opinion on the problem.

When he arrived at his office, Scott greeted his secretary, Joanne Evans, and asked her to call in the CFO, Joe Rayner.

A few minutes later, a gray-haired gentleman in his sixties walked into Scott's office.

Scott greeted Rayner as the two men sat down.

"Why do you think Xcorp is in trouble?" asked Scott.

"I blame our lackluster performance on your predecessor," replied Rayner. "He expanded too quickly and diversified in too many areas. This forced us to go to the financial markets to raise capital at a time when the cost of money was high and the company's credit standing was deteriorating.

"I think the high cost of financing, along with a lack of expertise in the new areas we were moving into, led us to a situation where we were not competitive in meeting customer needs," stated Rayner.

The CFO's assessment came close to Scott's own view. Yet Scott was uneasy to hear the chief financial officer of the corporation putting the blame for financial problems on a person who was not there to defend his position. He thanked the CFO as he showed him out of his office.

The CFO's assessment may well have been correct, and Scott certainly knew how to begin to handle this type of situation—by zeroing in on profitability by product/service line and eliminating those lines that were not likely to contribute to the overall corporate bottom line. But he wanted to know more about why Xcorp had expanded into so many new areas, and why so many products were not successful.

Scott told his secretary that he wanted to see the vice-president of Xcorp's main manufacturing division.

Ten minutes later Tom Brown, a middle-aged man, was in the reception area waiting to go into Scott's office. He had been one of the key people on the old management team who was close to Scott's predecessor.

Brown knew that many Xcorp products were not doing well in the market. He also knew that many people were blaming his department. He was nervous and apprehensive as he walked into Scott's office and met the new CEO. He sat quietly waiting for Scott to begin the conversation.

"Tell me," asked the new CEO, "what is the real problem here at Xcorp?"

Brown felt threatened and became tense by the question.

"I inherited a lot of problems when I took over as vice-president of manufacturing. Since then our situation has become much better. The real problem is in the Sales Department. Sales are down and erratic. That causes us to keep adjusting our production schedule on short notice. The salesmen promise delivery without checking with us, and they don't get all the information we need to schedule production until the last minute. With the current situation it is impossible to have meaningful production planning. And with poor production planning, we can't keep the machines fully occupied. This is why we have excessive downtime."

Scott heard what Brown was saying but could not understand why the manufacturing and sales departments had not got their acts together. He thanked Brown as he led him to the door, and then he called in the vice-president of Sales.

Peter Clark was not exactly what Scott had expected. In contrast with the nervous and defensive posture Brown had portrayed, Clark was bursting with enthusiasm.

"Why is Xcorp in trouble?" asked Scott.

"Sir, I think our major problems are the poor quality of our products and the late shipment of goods to the customer. Many of our customers expect 'just-in-time' delivery so they can control their inventories, and we let them down repeatedly. We have lost many customers for these two reasons. You see, my department is the contact between the customer and the company. We take the heat when the customer is upset. I see too many boxes of defective products returned to us for shipment to our plants. And some of these were products the customer had to wait to receive for more than thirty days past the promised date of shipment."

Clark's remarks made Scott realize the scope of the difficulties Xcorp was facing. He had many questions to ask Clark but decided to save them for a later date. He thanked Clark for his input.

Scott decided that lack of communication, finger pointing, and refusal to accept responsibility were among the symptoms plaguing the company.

Scott realized that he needed more detailed and reliable information. He called Joanne Evans to his office.

"For one week," he instructed her, "I want to see every piece of paper that comes across your desk."

"Certainly, sir, and here is a list of people who have asked to see you."

"Thank you, but I don't want to get bogged down in meetings during the first week. I want you to help me get to know this company."

Evans smiled. "I'll do my best. How would you like to begin?" she asked.

"To start with, please arrange a suitable time for the head of Data Processing to come to see me."

"That will be Ken Johnson."

Evans left Scott's office and returned shortly carrying a large stack of correspondence. She set the stack on Scott's desk. "Happy reading!" she said with a sympathetic smile.

One hour later Ken Johnson arrived.

"I am hoping that you are the one person who can help me out," said Scott. "I need information about our products, our services, our customers, and our market share."

Johnson was a methodical person. He had spent the previous fifteen years in data processing. "Let me write down the categories of information that you need, and I'll be happy to put a report together for you," said Johnson.

"First, I want to know about the financial status of all our units," Scott instructed him. "For example, is each plant making or losing money? Was the last quarter typical for each plant? How did it compare with the same quarter over the past few years?

"Second, I need specific information on the efficiency of our operation, and the quality of our products as perceived by the customer.

"Third, I would like to know about our sales and market share and how our products compare with the competition.

"Fourth, I am interested in unit price and unit costs of our products broken down by their major cost components."

Johnson carefully wrote down these requests. As the list grew longer and longer, his face became more and more serious. He asked Scott, "Do you want to know all of this information about each of your divisions and plants?"

"Yes, of course!" exclaimed Scott.

"I'll see what I can do," said Johnson.

"When will you have it ready?" asked Scott.

"Well," replied Johnson, "I will have to do a brief study to determine how long it will take. It may take several weeks. I'm not sure."

"But I want this information tomorrow!" exclaimed Scott.

"It is impossible to put together a report like this for you by tomorrow. You are asking some questions that people haven't asked before. We just aren't equipped to give you instant answers."

"You're not providing this type of information already? Don't you have any reports that I could look at?"

"Yes, we do," said Johnson. "I was going to pull the information out of the various reports and make a special summary for you. And that would take time—a lot of time."

"Send me the reports as they are," directed Scott. "I'll go through them myself."

"I can certainly do that by tomorrow." Johnson shook hands and left Scott's office.

Scott went to his desk and blocked out the next morning on his calendar. He walked to his secretary's area. "I'd like to see the human resources director, Gail Locke, next."

Ten minutes later Scott opened the door to welcome an elegant woman in her early forties. He offered her a chair and proceeded directly to the point.

"You and I both know that it is the people that make or break an organization. I like to see our people involved and motivated. I want them to work with me as a team. Therefore, I need to get to know them, and I need you to help me."

Locke was pleased. Scott was talking her language. She smiled.

"Before we do anything to introduce change, I've got to know what is going on," continued Scott. "I need information about our people. For example, how many employees are there in the various units, divisions, and plants of this corporation? What is the employee mix by race and sex, and what is the average salary for different grades? When was the last time employees received a raise, and were the raises based on performance? Most important, who are the great performers in this company and how are they rewarded for their performance? I want a comprehensive answer."

Locke looked puzzled as she asked, "Do you want to reward people when the company is in trouble?"

"Yes!" replied Scott emphatically. "I know the company is losing money. But that doesn't mean we don't have great performers. I want to know all the real stars, not just a few people who were lucky enough to have exposure. I want to know who really deserves the credit."

"You want all that information from me?" Locke exclaimed.

"Who else can I ask? You are more in touch with our people than anyone else, or you should be."

Locke was at a loss. Scott noticed her uneasiness and realized he was asking too much.

"I'll settle for this. Put together all the information you can find, and let's see what we have."

"Okay," she agreed doubtfully. "How soon do you want this?"

"Tomorrow," said Scott.

"I'll see what I can do by tomorrow afternoon."

"That will be fine," replied Scott as he saw Gail Locke out of the office and said good-bye.

WHEN Scott returned from lunch, he found a huge pile of papers on the corner of his desk. "What is all this?" he asked his secretary.

"The first batch of correspondence and reports that have come to my desk this afternoon," she replied. "And according to your wishes, I am putting everything on your desk."

He sat at his desk and began going through the papers. About halfway down the stack, he noticed something odd—the shortest letter he had ever seen. It read, "Dear Mr. Scott: I can help you solve your information problem." And that was it. Scott chuckled as he threw the letter in the wastebasket and continued with his reading.

Ten minutes later, Scott was searching through his basket to read the letter again.

"How did this guy know I have an information problem?" he wondered. He found the letter and looked at it again. It was signed "The Infoman." He threw it back in the wastebasket with a sigh. "I wish it were signed 'Superman.'"

Scott spent the rest of the afternoon working his way through the correspondence and reports.

TUESDAY promised to be an exciting day for Scott. He arrived at the office eager to go over all the reports Johnson and Locke were going to bring him.

At 8:00 sharp, Johnson knocked at Scott's door and brought in twenty binders of reports, each about two inches thick. He said, "These are financial reports for each division for the last month. If you want the breakdowns at the plant level, there are a hundred reports like this in my office. I'll have them brought in. I'll also bring you the operation reports in a few minutes."

Johnson left Scott's room and returned with a trolley carrying stacks of thick computer reports. He carefully placed them in a neat row on Scott's conference table, then turned and walked out.

Scott was in shock when he saw the masses of reports. He had expected to see several reports but not quite so many. He couldn't make sense out of this much information even if he could force himself to go through all the reports.

"I can't wade through this mass of data in search of the pertinent facts I require," he thought, realizing that his plan for learning what was going on by examining reports was not going to work. It would take months to understand the contents of these reports.

Scott made a cursory survey of several binders before he gave up.

Information overload was causing him to forget the key questions he had asked the previous day. He sat down and took a deep breath to regain control.

Scott's eyes fell upon a personal computer near his desk. Surely, through this computer it must be possible to pull out the pertinent information he needed, not just masses of numbers. He called his secretary.

"Do you know how to use the computer in here?"

"No, sir. I have never used it."

"Who knows how to use this computer?"

"A gentleman in data processing who is no longer with the company installed it eight months ago. But I'm sure there is someone in the company who knows how it works," she said. "Let me check around."

"Who has been using this computer in the last eight months?"

"No one. The past president of the company didn't like personal computers," stated Joanne Evans.

"Then why did he have it in his office?"

"It was first brought here for a demonstration. Later, a decision was made to provide personal computers to all the top executives," she replied.

"Who made that decision?"

"The decision was made by the Computer Steering Committee."

Scott dialed Johnson's number. "I have a personal computer in my office," he said. "Could you send someone over to show me how to use it? Maybe I can get information from the machine instead of going through all the reports you sent me. That will save me time."

"We'll be right up," said Johnson. "I'm glad to hear you're interested in computers."

Half an hour later, Johnson and a young man arrived at Scott's office.

The young assistant turned the machine on to demonstrate its features. "With this machine," he said, "you can do word processing, a way of typing that allows easy editing of what you have typed for final printing. You can do spread-sheet calculations for constructing a budget and a forecast. Also, there is a program in this machine for creating files."

The explanation was not making an impact on Scott. He was interested neither in word processing nor in creating his own budgets and forecasts. He was even less interested in creating his own files.

"What else can this machine do?" asked Scott. "Can I specify what I want and get the answer on the screen?"

"It depends on what you specify, sir," said Johnson's assistant.

"We've been working on connecting these personal computers to our main computer," said Johnson, "to allow you to ask limited questions and receive the answer. But that project is not ready right now."

"When will it be ready?" asked Scott.

"We have scheduled it for the third quarter of next year."

Scott paused for a minute and asked, "What else can this machine do?"

"Sir, it does what we have shown you and it will do a lot more in the future."

Scott was angry. He looked at Johnson and asked, "Are we still buying these computers?"

"Yes," was the answer. "We are buying them for the people who need them."

"Well, I don't need one," said Scott, fighting to keep his voice down. "Instead of buying another unit, take mine and give it to whoever needs it."

"Yes, sir," replied Johnson. He and his assistant left the president's office carrying Scott's computer.

Scott was upset. It occurred to him that his plan for finding out what was going on was actually unfolding. He knew that what he was experiencing was typical of many businesses where people get caught up in everyday routines and rarely ask questions. Yet his basic questions remained unanswered, and time was not standing still.

There was a knock at the door. It was Gail Locke.

"I have some of the information you were seeking, Mr. Scott," she said.

"Come in and sit down," said Scott.

Locke looked at Scott. "You seem disturbed. Is anything wrong?" she asked.

"Yes," replied Scott. "But I don't yet know what the problem is. Tell me, what have you got?"

"Well, let me say first that I don't have all the information you asked for. I can tell you the numbers of people we have employed. I can give you some idea of the socioeconomic mix. I can't tell you who is doing what, who is a good performer and who is not. There are just too many people. We don't seem to have a way to get that kind of answer, even though we have a performance-appraisal system.

"I have put together whatever information I could find relevant to the concerns you raised yesterday. These four binders will provide answers to some of your questions. Please call me if I can be of any additional help."

Locke placed four binders on Scott's desk and left the room.

The president stood up and paced back and forth. He looked at the stack of reports and binders that were surrounding him, then sat down and closed his eyes.

He wanted to find the key information, but how? When he opened his eyes, he glanced at an Xcorp organization chart on the wall. He saw that he was ten levels removed from the company's first-line supervisors. Unless he became better informed on what was happening at those ten levels, how could he even know if ten levels were necessary?

With a sigh, he went back to his desk to review the correspondence he had received that day. He began working his way through the stack.

Suddenly he came across a letter that looked similar to the one he had seen the day before. It was noticeably brief and had no return address or telephone number. It said, "Dear Mr. Scott: Don't give up. I can help you solve your information problem." Signed, "The Infoman."

Scott was curious. "Infoman," he thought. "Give me a break! How does this guy know that I have this problem or that I'm about to give up? Is he some George Burns type character?" He called his secretary.

"Do you know someone called the Infoman?" he inquired.

"Info who?" she asked.

"Infoman," said Scott.

"I'm afraid I've never heard of him," replied Evans, trying not to laugh.

"Oh, well," thought Scott, "miracles are hard to come by." He went back to his piles of paper.

That afternoon the secretary's phone rang. "Could I speak to Mr. Scott?" a pleasant voice asked.

"I'm sorry. He's still at lunch. Whom shall I say called?" asked Evans.

"Tell him the Infoman," replied the voice.

Evans began to laugh. "If this is some kind of joke, I don't think you'll find Mr. Scott in a very receptive mood right now."

"I know that," said the Infoman. "That's why I'm calling. I will be in your area next Thursday and I'd like to stop by at nine A.M. to see him. Do you have the authority to make an appointment for Mr. Scott?"

"Yes," said Evans, a little taken aback by the assertiveness of this mysterious person.

She checked Scott's calendar for the time requested. It was blank. So Evans went ahead and wrote in the appointment book: "The Infoman."

"I can't wait until Thursday," she thought to herself.

On Thursday morning promptly at 9:00 A.M., a well-dressed man walked up to Scott's secretary and introduced himself as the Infoman.

"Good morning, Mr. Infoman," replied Evans with a smile. "Mr. Scott is expecting you."

The Infoman smiled back. "I'm glad to be here," he said. He looked dignified, calm, and self-assured. He knocked and entered Scott's office.

Scott was sitting at his desk, busy with that day's papers that had accumulated on yesterday's pile. He stood up and greeted the Infoman cautiously.

"When I got your two notes, I didn't know whether you were real or just some prankster," said Scott.

"That's just as well," said the Infoman. "I'm glad you kept an open mind." The two men sat down.

"So you can solve all my problems!" commented Scott sarcastically.

"No, but I can help you with your information problem," replied the Infoman confidently.

"Please tell me how."

The Infoman paused for a few moments. He saw the stack of reports on Scott's conference table and the piles of paper on his desk. He looked at Scott and said, "Before I explain how, I'd like to ask you a question."

"**F**IRE away," said Scott.

"What do you perceive your information problem to be?" asked the Infoman.

Scott pointed at the stacks of reports and papers in his office. "You see all of these," he said. "They are only a fraction of the information available in this company. I don't have the time to go through even these, let alone all the other reports that are not here."

"Do you feel you need to go through them?" asked the Infoman.

"I sure do," said Scott, "at least once, to know what we have to work with. How else can I find out what is going on?"

The Infoman's face brightened. "I like that," he said. "Many presidents rely exclusively on subordinates to tell them what is going on." He then paused for emphasis and said, "I'm glad you want to . . ."

*

Find
Out
The
Truth
For
Yourself

*

Scott felt good about the Infoman's compliment. He was seeking the truth for himself because he knew that painting a picture of what was going on based solely on the impressions of others would give him a view of the company that could be far from reality.

"Do you understand my information problem now?" asked Scott.

"I am beginning to," said the Infoman. "Tell me this. Assuming that I can help, what would you like me to do?"

"Well, if you could help me digest all of these reports quickly to discover our real problems and opportunities, you would be a hero. But I know you can't. It just isn't possible."

The Infoman was listening attentively. After a thoughtful pause, he smiled and spoke with great confidence. "I believe you have a double information problem. Your first problem is getting to know a new and large company quickly, to find out what's going on.

"After you solve that problem, you'll be better informed, but the information overload will not go away. As soon as the new set of reports starts to pile up, your problem will reappear. The second information problem, therefore, is to stay abreast of what's going on. I'm sure your people also share this problem.

"Your situation," continued the Infoman, "brings to mind the image of a person drowning in a sea of information. Suppose all around you was information. How could you save your life?"

"I'd probably try to read as much as I could, as quickly as possible."

"Exactly," said the Infoman. "What would happen if you drank as much water as you could as quickly as possible in the sea?"

"I would drown," said Scott.

"Then why doesn't a fish drown when it's swimming around all the time in a potentially drowning environment?" asked the Infoman.

"Because," he continued, "it has gills, a built-in screening system to help it take from the water only what it needs and leave what it doesn't need."

"That's exactly right!" exclaimed Scott. "I need a system that can screen all this data and give me only what I need."

"Let me suggest that this screening system is the solution to your information problem. Furthermore, all the key information you need to manage your people can be summarized in three One Page Reports."

"One page! That's ridiculous!" Scott scoffed at the idea. "How big are these One Page Reports?"

The Infoman smiled and replied. "Regular eight and a half by eleven sheets."

"That's just not possible. I've got all these reports to go through, and if I ever got through them, I'd probably still feel I didn't have enough good information. How can you imagine that all of this information can possibly be reduced to a single One Page Report?"

"You need THREE One Page Reports," said the Infoman as he handed Scott a piece of paper.

THE THREE ONE PAGE REPORTS

REPORT 1—FOCUS REPORT

The key information about WHAT YOU DO

REPORT 2—FEEDBACK REPORT

The GOOD NEWS and the BAD NEWS about
WHAT YOU DO

REPORT 3—MANAGEMENT REPORT

The GOOD NEWS and the BAD NEWS about
WHAT YOUR PEOPLE DO

As Scott was studying the sheet, the Infoman began to explain it.

"The First One Page Report focuses you on the key information that is relevant to you and your job. This report is tailor-made for you. Your One Page Report will not be meaningful to anyone else in the company because no one else does what you do. I call this the FOCUS REPORT.

"The Second One Page Report gives you feedback on your performance. It highlights the good news and bad news from your first report. The Second One Page Report is briefer than your first report because news that is neither good nor bad doesn't appear. I call this the FEEDBACK REPORT.

"The Third One Page Report gives you all the good news and bad news about your people. It gives you a view of what's happening below you down through each layer of the organization. I call this report the MANAGEMENT REPORT."

Scott liked the concept of the three One Page Reports. "I can see how valuable such reports would be," he said. "But who prepares these reports?"

"Managers decide what information they need—I'll explain how this is done later. The information is then gathered, screened, and organized either manually or by the computer. Of course, the larger the organization, the more sense it makes to use a computer."

"The computer is a mystery to me," said Scott jokingly, "although I'm aware of its potential value and I just bought one for my kids to play with."

The Infoman smiled. "I love the computer and you will too when it begins to give you the support you need.

"Let's look at it this way," continued the Infoman. "You probably know just as little about your television as you do about your computer, yet you use your TV all the time and don't see it as a mystery."

"That's true," said Scott.

"What would you do if none of the TV channels had a program that interested you?"

"I wouldn't watch it," replied Scott.

"That's exactly why you have not been using computers so far. Either there is no computer program that interests you, or there may be one that would interest you very much but you haven't seen it yet. One Page Management can become one such program. It'll hold the key to your survival in a 'sea of information.'"

Scott was intrigued. "Tell me more about this computer program," he said.

"As you know," said the Infoman, "the computer can be programmed to do the same things that a person preparing the reports would do. The computer is there as a tool, a helper. I'd certainly recommend it for a company this size.

"During my visits," continued the Infoman, "I will explain how the reports can be prepared manually. That way you'll know you've got a choice of keeping it manual, of getting your computer people to develop a program, or of purchasing the computer program known as The One Page System (TOPS). Whichever way you do it, the result is the same—three One Page Reports."

"Three One Page Reports instead of this huge stack in my office!" exclaimed Scott. "It's too good to be true. When can we start?"

"Why don't we start right away? You still have an information problem."

"Fine," confirmed Scott. "I'll assign this project to the head of Data Processing."

"I can see why you might want to do that," said the Infoman. "But it won't work. It's not fair to expect the computer department to do managers' job for them. Your managers should get involved themselves and you need to be involved in the project too."

Scott was startled by the Infoman's assertiveness.

"I can't afford the time to be involved personally. Xcorp has other serious problems besides the information problem," he said.

The Infoman smiled. "Let me suggest to you that your other serious problems are also related to information.

"First of all, if the right people had the right information at the right time, these problems would not be as serious as they are now. Second, as you begin to solve these serious problems, you need GOOD information to tell you how your solutions are working.

"Let me give you an example," continued the Infoman. "Suppose you develop a plan to drastically reduce the use of company credit cards and assign the implementation of this plan to a subordinate.

"Every time you ask him how this plan is working, you are seeking information. Your subordinate may not be carrying out your plan and may hide the truth by telling you that he* is working on it, when in fact, he is buying time until you ask the question again. He has that information; you don't. The fact that you don't allows him to procrastinate."

The Infoman's example could not have been more appropriate. Scott had just started a plan to control the use of company credit cards and was interested in its success.

Scott paused a few minutes to think over what the Infoman had said. He turned to the Infoman. With a nod he gave his assent and agreed to oversee the project personally. The starting date was set for Monday.

---

*For ease of reading, the male gender is used throughout the book.

THE Infoman arrived on time for his Monday appointment with Scott. Scott welcomed him. "I can't wait to hear more about how the three One Page Reports will solve our information problem," Scott began.

"They will solve your information problem by giving managers the key information they need," said the Infoman.

"But how does this screening system know what information our managers need?" asked Scott.

"The managers specify the information they need to help them succeed in their jobs."

The Infoman continued. "They need information to guide them to success. We must, therefore, examine different people's view of success and how their perceptions relate to information. Let's start with some broad definitions and then discuss specific applications."

The Infoman then gave Scott a sheet of paper that read:

*

*The Road to
Success
Is
Paved With
'Good Information'*

*

Scott laughed. "I certainly agree with that, but could you elaborate?"

"Of course," replied the Infoman. "Success obviously means different things to different people. Different folks have different goals. To some people success means making a lot of money. To others it may mean making an artistic contribution. Each person has his idea of success, and that's the right definition for that person." He paused. "What does success mean to you?" he asked Scott.

"To turn Xcorp around," was the immediate answer.

"That's great," said the Infoman. "You've just defined an important area of success for yourself, and I know you'll make it." He then took a piece of paper and wrote:

SUCCESS DEFINED FOR BRIAN SCOTT

SUCCESS AREA: Turn Xcorp Around

"Now, what most people don't realize is the importance of being able to recognize when they are successful—when they have actually arrived at their destination.

"Supposing that in a year Xcorp is turned around," continued the Infoman, "how would you know it has happened? What would you look at to show you that you have been successful?"

"Well, I would look at several factors."

"Let's write them down. What are your Success Factors?" asked the Infoman.

"I would look at my bottom line to see if we are profitable. That would be one indication. If we were increasingly selling more than our competitors and gaining in 'market share,' that would be another good indicator of success. If we were paying off our debt from revenues rather than assets to decrease our 'debt ratio,' that would be a good indicator. Of course, in my view, success for Xcorp would touch on many other areas as well, such as having a motivated, productive, and unified work force."

"I'd like to write these down," interrupted the Infoman. "I can see you have great plans for Xcorp, but for illustrating the concepts we are discussing, let's just take the first three factors that you mentioned."

The Infoman wrote on the piece of paper the indicators of success that Scott had enumerated. He labeled them SUCCESS FACTORS.

SUCCESS DEFINED FOR BRIAN SCOTT

SUCCESS AREA: Turn Xcorp Around

Success Factors

Profit per share
Market Share
Debt/Equity Ratio

The Infoman showed the list to Scott and said, "When I look at this list I wonder what your goals for these Success Factors are. For example, how profitable do you want the company to be before you'd consider yourself successful?"

"The Board of Directors told me," replied Scott, "that the stockholders would be satisfied with a profit per share of two dollars and a debt to equity ratio of point five. Regarding the market share, our existing manufacturing capacity can handle twenty percent of current demands for the major products we are producing."

The Infoman wrote the goals down on the same sheet of paper across from Scott's success factors.

SUCCESS DEFINED FOR BRIAN SCOTT

SUCCESS AREA: Turn Xcorp Around

Success Factors	*Goals*
Profit per share	$2.00
Market Share	20%
Debt/Equity Ratio	0.5

Scott looked at the list the Infoman had constructed and said, "This is only a partial list of success factors; I'd like to complete the list."

The Infoman felt good about Scott's level of interest. He was impressed with Scott's desire for thoroughness. "When you have completed the list," said the Infoman, "you will have defined many success factors, perhaps too many.

"Please remember to select only the most important ones and call them CRITICAL SUCCESS FACTORS."

The Infoman's question "How do you know if you have succeeded?" intrigued Scott, who was thinking of other indicators of success to add to the list.

When Scott looked up, the Infoman smiled and said, "The next step after defining Critical Success Factors is to relate them to information. Let me show you one of the notes I keep in my office."

*

*Watching
Your Progress
Will Keep You
On The Road
To
Success*

*

"You watch your progress," continued the Infoman, "by looking at GOOD INFORMATION. By Good Information I mean information that is accurate and relevant. For example, if your goal is to increase your profit per share, the fact that Xcorp profit per share was ten cents last quarter is good information. The fact that your brother's company made one dollar profit per share is irrelevant. The Good Information about your Critical Success Factor is called your STATUS.

"The information you really need from all these reports in your office is the Good Information I am talking about. It is the information that gives you your current Status on your profit per share, market share, and debt/equity ratio."

"I think I am beginning to see how all this fits together," said Scott with excitement. "Let me see if I can find my Status, or Good Information." He took the sheet of paper on which the Infoman had written down a few Success Factors. He walked to his conference table, took out several reports from the stack, and after spending some time, he extracted the information he needed and entered it under the heading marked Status. When he was finished, the chart read as follows:

SUCCESS DEFINED FOR BRIAN SCOTT

SUCCESS AREA: Turn Xcorp Around

Critical Success Factor	Status	Goal
Profit per share	Negative	$2.00
Market Share	10%	20%
Debt/Equity Ratio	0.9	0.5

The Infoman said, "Xcorp's Status doesn't look that great, which explains why you have been recruited to this position. You see, what you just did helped us both see where you are compared to your goals. It communicated accurate information to both of us."

It was noon. Scott and the Infoman decided to break for lunch. They walked around the corner to Scott's favorite restaurant. While they were enjoying their food, the Infoman noticed that Scott was in a pensive mood.

"Tell me what's bothering you," urged the Infoman.

"I understand everything we have gone through this morning," said Scott. "I can see how Critical Success Factors are defined by the individual. What I am worried about is groups!"

"Groups?" queried the Infoman. "Why should that bother you?"

"Well, it seems to me everything is going to get a lot more complicated when people are in groups, as we almost always are. For example, consider a family. My son Mark may choose a Success Area—to become the best basketball player in his school. He may define his own Critical Success Factors and watch his progress toward his own goals as you have described.

"Meanwhile," added Scott, "I as his father don't happen to agree with his priority when I see that his preoccupation with sports is causing him to flunk out of high school. It may be much more important to me that he keep his grades up so that he can get into a good university. How do my wishes come into the picture?

Similarly, "In a company environment," continued Scott, "people interact with other people. What one person considers success may not be on target with the overall goals of the corporation. Doesn't that make the whole thing more complex?"

The Infoman was nodding his head. "I understand your concern. "That's a smart observation. But believe it or not, I have thought of this situation and have devised FOUR SIMPLE STEPS to handle the problem. I'd be happy to discuss them now, or when we get back to the office."

"Let's talk about it at the office," said Scott. "In the meantime, enjoy your lunch."

Back at the office, the Infoman began to describe the Four Simple Steps for ensuring that a person's success will also lead to group success.

"You'll see," said the Infoman, "that the discussions this morning about success will be particularly useful in explaining the Four Simple Steps." The Infoman showed Scott a sheet of paper that read:

**THE FOUR SIMPLE STEPS
TO DEFINE
CRITICAL SUCCESS FACTORS**

Step 1

KNOW YOUR IMPORTANT RELATIONSHIPS

Step 2

DEFINE SUCCESS AREAS FOR YOURSELF FROM
SEVERAL VIEWPOINTS

Step 3

IDENTIFY CRITICAL SUCCESS FACTORS FOR EACH
SUCCESS AREA

Step 4

DETERMINE WHERE TO FIND STATUS OF EACH
CRITICAL SUCCESS FACTOR

AS Scott finished reading the slip of paper, the Infoman said, "Let me explain these steps in more detail. The first step is to identify important RELATIONSHIPS. These relationships consist of each manager's employer, his boss, the people who supply him with goods and services, and the people who receive the results or outputs of the manager's work. Anyone who receives and uses the outputs of the manager's job can be called a USER.

"The employer pays the salary, the boss provides ongoing supervision, the suppliers provide the materials to work with, and the users receive the fruits of the manager's work. In some cases, of course, the employer, the boss, and the user can be the same person."

"As the CEO, who would my users be?"

"Well," replied the Infoman, "let's list all the outputs of your job. You are in charge of Xcorp. The outputs of this company are its products. The customer is your user. Moreover, as the CEO, you generate plans, issue instructions, write memos and letters. Therefore, the people who receive these are also your users."

"That's a lot of people," said Scott.

"True, but they conveniently fit into the categories of customer, direct subordinates, and other staff."

"Why is it necessary to identify these relationships?" asked Scott.

"Because in a group setting, managers are expected to satisfy all these relationships. They've got to know who they are satisfying and why, and who they are not satisfying and why. The employer, boss, suppliers, and users often have different expectations. Bosses may be interested in getting the job done fast, while users have interest in quality and on-time delivery. And the employer wants the manager to save or make enough money to justify his salary."

Scott was pleased with the Infoman's answer. "This wasn't hard," he said. "What's the next step?"

"The second step is defining SUCCESS AREAS. Managers define success from their own points of view as well as from the viewpoints of their users, suppliers, employers, and bosses. Unless these people have exactly the same point of view, the manager will end up with several Success Areas, such as Improving Timeliness, Quality, and Reducing Costs.

"The third step is to define SUCCESS FACTORS for each Success Area. It involves asking the question 'How do I know I have succeeded?' This question will lead managers to identify a list of Success Factors for each Success Area. Examples of Success Factors are Percent First Quality, Percent Deadlines Met, and Percent Turnover. The manager should negotiate with his boss to select the most important Success Factors that cover all his relationships. The result will be a list of Critical Success Factors in a group setting."

What the Infoman was saying made a lot of sense to Scott. He wanted his people to go through these steps so they would become focused on the critical issues he was concerned about such as customer satisfaction and cost containment.

"Tell me about the Fourth Simple Step," requested Scott.

"The fourth step is simple but time-consuming the first time it is done. It involves studying the available data to determine how to find information about the STATUS of the Critical Success Factors just defined. To perform this step, managers should collect all the reports available to them including those they create and those they receive.

"Managers should particularly seek out reports generated in their user areas containing information about their work. After collecting these reports, they should examine them to determine where Good Information could be found. If information for a Critical Success Factor doesn't exist, then managers should estimate the value of having that information, and arrange to have data available if it is worth the effort."

The Infoman looked at his watch. It was time to leave. "We've discussed the Four Simple Steps," he said, "that will help your managers identify the information they need to succeed at work. This type of information makes up the One Page Reports. I'll show you a sample of the First Report, the FOCUS REPORT, next Thursday if you are free. Why don't you spend some time thinking about your Critical Success Factors before we meet next week?"

PART II

One Page Management

IT was Thursday morning. As Scott was preparing for his meeting with the Infoman, his secretary informed him that the Infoman had arrived. The Infoman was as full of energy and enthusiasm as before. He greeted Scott warmly.

"I am aware that I have made a lot of promises about One Page Management," said the Infoman. "Today I'd like to start delivering on them. Let me summarize my promises. When we first met, you were suffering from information overload."

"I sure was," said Scott, "and still am!"

"I proposed a screening system that would take from the sea of information only the good information each manager needed, and would leave the rest. I suggested that the screening system would give each manager three One Page Reports containing only what that person required.

"Today I'd like to begin describing the specifics of the three One Page Reports. Let's begin with the first one, the FOCUS REPORT."

"I can't believe we are actually going to see the mysterious One Page Report," Scott remarked jokingly.

The Infoman smiled. He opened his briefcase and took out a pad of paper. "Let's begin by reviewing the Critical Success Factors we discussed before. I'll show you how they fit into the One Page Report."

Scott had defined other Critical Success Factors since his last meeting with the Infoman. He showed his notes to the Infoman. Scott explained how he had applied the Four Simple Steps and had come up with the Success Areas of Sales, Production, Distribution, and Financial. The Infoman and Scott both looked at the Critical Success Factors that Scott had defined for those Success Areas. When they finished, the Infoman arranged the information on the pad of paper and showed it to Scott.

BUSINESS SUCCESS DEFINED FOR BRIAN SCOTT

SUCCESS AREA 1—**SALES**

Critical Success Factors	Status	Goal
Market Share	10%	20%
Implement New Sales		
Program—Phase I	Planning	April 1

SUCCESS AREA 2—**PRODUCTION**

Critical Success Factors	Status	Goal
First Quality	92%	98%
Identify Unprofitable		
Product Lines	Planning	March 1

SUCCESS AREA 3—**DISTRIBUTION**

Critical Success Factors	Status	Goal
Inventory Turnover		
per Month	3	8
Liquidate Dead		
Inventory	Planning	March 1

SUCCESS AREA 4—**FINANCIAL**

Critical Success Factors	Status	Goal
Profit per Share	Negative	$2.00
Debt/Equity Ratio	0.9	0.5
Staff Reduction	Planning	March 1

"**T**HIS sheet of paper will help you focus on the status of your Critical Success Factors and tells you how far you are from your goals. It looks to me like you are pretty far."

"I sure am," confirmed Scott with a sigh.

"I didn't mean to discourage you. I know that these are tough goals.

"You have specified one goal for each of these Critical Success Factors. You need three," said the Infoman.

Scott looked puzzled. "Why three?" he wondered.

"The first goal level is the minimum limit. The second is the satisfactory target, and the third is the outstanding target."

"The MINIMUM LEVEL is the borderline between satisfactory and unacceptable. It is important for people to know at what point they consider their status unacceptable."

"Wouldn't a single standard indicate that?"

"Not really," replied the Infoman. "A single standard generally sets the ultimate goal for a Critical Success Factor, not the bare minimum. To illustrate the point, let me ask you to remember a Critical Success Factor that you were responsible for when you were a plant manager."

Scott reflected and said, "Percent of scheduled time our machines were running."

"Okay," said the Infoman. "What was the single standard you had?"

"Of course, our goal was high—ninety-eight percent," replied Scott proudly.

"What was your status when you left that job?"

Scott reflected and replied, "Well, we were averaging eighty-nine percent."

"Was eighty-nine percent acceptable?"

"Yes, anywhere above eighty-five percent was acceptable, but we were shooting for ninety-eight percent."

"That's just the point," said the Infoman. "I consider eighty-five percent to be the Minimum Level, the first of the three goal levels."

"What would the other two goal levels be then?"

The Infoman said, "Before I answer that question, tell me how many times you achieved your ultimate standard?"

"We never made it, but came close," replied Scott.

"How did you feel about never making your goal?"

"Frustrated," replied Scott. "We felt we could make it if everything went smoothly and our maintenance department was on its toes."

The Infoman pointed to Scott's desk. He said, "If my goal is to get to your desk from here, I should not feel bad because my first step was not big enough to get me there. That is quite a jump in an office as big as yours. I must take a few steps and feel good after each step. The second goal level, the SATISFACTORY GOAL LEVEL, is the next achievable step that would satisfy you that you are heading toward your ultimate goal. In your example, it could be ninety-two percent."

"We made that a few times during my last year at the job," said Scott.

"Great. Did you feel good about it?"

"We sure did," affirmed Scott.

"The third goal level is the OUTSTANDING GOAL LEVEL. This is the achievable but challenging target that in most cases is achieved over a long period of time. In your case, ninety-eight percent would be the Outstanding Goal. Outstanding goals are usually attained through a series of Satisfactory steps.

"Tough goals can be accomplished one step at a time. This is why I recommend the three goal levels.

"Let me summarize," continued the Infoman. "The Outstanding Goal Level is the ultimate and achievable goal. The Satisfactory Goal Level is the next achievable goal. When you make this goal, you should feel good. If you don't, it means you have not defined it to be challenging enough. The Minimum Level is borderline performance. When you perform worse than this minimum, you know you're in trouble."

The Infoman looked at the sheet of paper that contained Scott's Critical Success Factors and said, "The three goal levels will have a different interpretation for the projects you have listed here such as implementing a new sales program. I know your target deadline is April first. That would be your Outstanding Goal Level. Now what would be a more comfortable, yet challenging, deadline for this project?"

Scott reflected for a few minutes and said, "I think May fifteenth would be satisfactory, although I prefer to have this project completed by April first."

"In that case, May fifteenth could be the Satisfactory Goal Level."

The Infoman continued, "What would be the latest date you would accept the completion of that project?"

"If the first phase of the new sales program is not in by May thirtieth, we will lose the opportunity of preparing ourselves for the summer sales campaign," asserted Scott.

"The Minimum Level for this project would therefore be May thirtieth" was the Infoman's response.

The Infoman looked again at the sheet of paper that contained Scott's Critical Success Factors. He worked with Scott to come up with three goal levels for each Critical Success Factor and entered the goals on the sheet of paper. When he was finished, he handed the first draft of Scott's Focus Report back to him. This report looked as follows:

THE FIRST ONE PAGE REPORT FOR
BRIAN SCOTT

Week Ending January 20

Critical Success Factors	*Status*	*Minimum Level*	*Satisfactory Goal Level*	*Outstanding Goal Level*

SUCCESS AREA 1—**SALES**

Market Share Implement New Sales Program—	10%	12%	15%	20%
Phase I	Planning	May 30	May 15	April 1

SUCCESS AREA 2—**PRODUCTION**

First Quality Identify Unprofitable	92%	90%	95%	98%
Lines	Planning	May 15	May 1	March 1

SUCCESS AREA 3—**DISTRIBUTION**

Inventory Turnover per Month Liquidate Dead	3	2	5	8
Inventory	Planning	May 1	April 1	March 1

SUCCESS AREA 4—**FINANCIAL**

Profit per Share	Negative	$0.5	$1.0	$2.0
Debt/Equity Ratio	0.9	0.7	0.6	0.5
Staff Reduction	Planning	May 1	March 30	March 1

Scott studied the sheet of paper. He was pleased. "The concept of three goal levels now seems so obvious to me that it is difficult to imagine ever operating without it!" commented Scott as he made a note on his pad that read "All good performance starts with clear goals."

"Goal setting is an important key to turning around Xcorp," said Scott. "We will implement your goal-setting system."

"I am pleased that you think so highly of the three goal levels. It's going to be exciting to see this goal-setting system at work here. Now I want to show you another part of the Focus Report. It deals with the TRENDS in the data."

Scott's curiosity increased. He had been using trend analysis for years as a way of interpreting historical data. He was interested to hear what the Infoman had to say.

The Infoman took from his briefcase a sample graph representing the performance of a typical Critical Success Factor of a foreman in a manufacturing plant. He showed the graph to Scott.

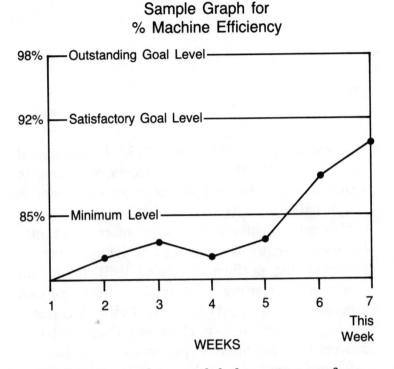

Sample Graph for
% Machine Efficiency

"Let's suppose this graph belongs to one of your people, say Turner. What is the graph telling you?"

"The first thing it shows me is that Turner's performance has been acceptable only in the last two weeks," replied Scott.

"Do you get any other information out of this graph?"

"Well, the graph indicates that Turner is heading in the right direction. He is getting closer to his goals, although he has not yet achieved his Satisfactory Goal Level."

"Exactly," said the Infoman. "This is very useful information. On the road to success, you have to know if you're headed in the right direction. A graph will illustrate that clearly.

"We can transfer this type of information onto the Focus Report by entering a 'G' for a good trend or improving performance, and a 'B' for a bad trend or worsening performance in a column labeled 'Trend' next to each Critical Success Factor. You will notice, of course, that the trend concept does not apply to projects such as the new sales program."

The Infoman discussed the past performance of Scott's Critical Success Factors with him and entered trend information where appropriate. When he had finished, he showed the pad to Scott saying, "This is an example of the Focus Report."

THE FOCUS REPORT FOR
BRIAN SCOTT

Week Ending January 20

Critical Success Factors	Status	Minimum Level	Satisfactory Goal Level	Outstanding Goal Level	Trend

SUCCESS AREA 1—SALES

Critical Success Factors	Status	Minimum Level	Satisfactory Goal Level	Outstanding Goal Level	Trend
Market Share	10%	12%	15%	20%	B
Implement New Sales Program— Phase I	Planning	May 30	May 15	April 1	—

SUCCESS AREA 2—PRODUCTION

Critical Success Factors	Status	Minimum Level	Satisfactory Goal Level	Outstanding Goal Level	Trend
First Quality	92%	90%	95%	98%	B
Identify Unprofitable Lines	Planning	May 15	May 1	March 1	—

SUCCESS AREA 3—DISTRIBUTION

Critical Success Factors	Status	Minimum Level	Satisfactory Goal Level	Outstanding Goal Level	Trend
Inventory Turnover per Month	3	2	5	8	B
Liquidate Dead Inventory	Planning	May 1	April 1	March 1	—

SUCCESS AREA 4—FINANCIAL

Critical Success Factors	Status	Minimum Level	Satisfactory Goal Level	Outstanding Goal Level	Trend
Profit per Share	Negative	$0.5	$1.0	$2.0	B
Debt/Equity Ratio	0.9	0.7	0.6	0.5	B
Staff Reduction	Planning	May 1	March 30	March 1	—

"To summarize, the first column is where you list all the Critical Success Factors you have defined. These factors should cover all your major areas of responsibility. The Critical Success Factors of each person should be unique and relevant to that person. In the second column you enter the status of your Critical Success Factors from the numerous reports available within the corporation. This column has the Good Information you need from the sea of information. The third, fourth, and fifth columns are your goals. In the sixth column you enter the trend information based on a historical graph of that Critical Success Factor."

Scott was thinking to himself how easy his job would be if all his managers looked at goal setting in this way—on a One Page Report. It would clarify accountability and performance standards, and encourage progress toward goals.

When Scott looked up, the Infoman was preparing to leave. "We've listed only a few of your Critical Success Factors to illustrate the concepts of the Focus Report. I suggest you spend time to complete this report yourself. I will be back when you have revised this report to move ahead to the next step in One Page Management." He shook hands with Scott and left the office.

It was noon. Scott decided to have lunch alone to think through his morning. He reflected on his visit with the Infoman. Opposing thoughts passed through his mind. Perhaps he, as the CEO of this corporation, could not afford to spend time on information and reports. Perhaps he should just concentrate on those short-term solutions he had started to implement that held the promise of success. Then he wouldn't need to spend hours constructing the One Page Report the Infoman was describing. He could get on with the urgent matters important to the Board of Directors. The thought became stronger and stronger. He was hungry.

After a good meal, Scott felt better about what he had heard that morning. He knew that the Infoman's system held significant possibilities and could even be the key to a long-term cure. He decided to make a commitment to implement One Page Management. He made a note of the commitment in his calendar to remember the date. He drafted a memo to start his people thinking about One Page Management. The memo said, "All memos circulating within Xcorp should not exceed one page. If it can't be said on one page, think of a simpler way of saying it."

UPON returning to his office, Scott distributed his memo. He then dialed a number and asked Brown, the vice-president of one of Xcorp's major manufacturing divisions, whom he had seen on his first day at Xcorp, to come to his office. He wanted to share with him what he had learned from the Infoman and to discuss the possibility of starting One Page Management in Brown's area.

Brown joined Scott and listened to his explanation of One Page Management, but he was not impressed. His reaction was cool and skeptical. "We are doing all this already," he said. "Besides, we have so many things going on that One Page Management should not be a priority at this time."

"What do you have going on?" asked Scott.

"Well, we are retooling plants and computerizing our manufacturing process from shop floor to shipping."

"That's an impressive agenda. How much of it is already done?"

"Quite a bit," replied Brown, "and that's why we shouldn't start anything new until we've finished what we've started."

"That sounds reasonable. When will it be finished?" asked Scott.

"The program has another two years to go."

Scott started to get angry. "You mean to tell me that you are not ready to begin anything new for the next two years? Then what am I here for? I have two years to turn this company around! I certainly won't stand by as an observer. I intend to implement change."

Brown kept quiet for a few minutes and then responded. "I didn't mean it that way," he said. "I am open to new ideas, but what I heard from you about One Page Management didn't strike me as anything new. We are doing it already."

"Tell me," said Scott, "what are your Critical Success Factors?"

"What do you mean?" asked Brown.

"I mean results that would indicate that your manufacturing division is doing a good job," continued Scott.

"There are quite a few," replied Brown.

"Can you tell me what they are?" asked Scott.

"I can give you a few, but to list them all, I have to look at our computer reports. It won't be one page; it's more like two hundred pages."

"There you are," said Scott. "Wouldn't you prefer to have it all on one page?"

"That's insane," replied Brown. "If I only look at one page, things will get out of hand."

"Out of whose hand?" asked Scott.

"You know what I mean," replied Brown.

Scott smiled, realizing what was worrying Brown. "You're right," he said. "Many things will get out of your hand, but that's where they belong. They belong to six hundred managers and supervisors who report to you directly or indirectly.

"Look, let's say your Critical Success Factors are in fact two hundred pages long. If you distribute the responsibility and control of these among your six hundred managers, there will be a third of one page for each person. Now, I know this is simplistic, but it demonstrates the point."

Scott's argument was not having the right effect on Brown. It was making him nervous and defensive.

"Do you have goals for your Critical Success Factors?" asked Scott.

"I do for the important ones," said Brown.

"And are managers below you, all the way down to the hourly workers, aware of their own Critical Success Factors, and do they have goals defined for each?"

"I'm not sure," said Brown. "How does that help with our efficiency and quality problems that are clearly machine related?"

"They may be machine related," was Scott's reply, "but machines are run by people, and it is people's work and creativity that we need to move forward."

"I agree," said Brown. "We need hardworking people. That's why I have gotten rid of many employees and supervisors during the last year. I can't stand people who are slow and expect to get paid without doing work."

Brown continued, "I believe we are getting maximum productivity out of our people now. The only other way to improve is to upgrade the machinery."

Scott was disturbed by Brown's statements. He realized that Brown's thinking was miles away from his own. He decided to keep an eye on Brown.

Scott paused and then said, "I have a distinct feeling that One Page Management can have a profound impact on this company. But I need somewhere to start using it."

"I think the sales area can really use this kind of program," replied Brown quickly, hoping Scott would leave him alone.

"I was hoping you would volunteer your area," suggested Scott.

"What is it exactly that you want me to do?" asked Brown.

"I want you and your managers to produce One Page Reports for yourselves so everyone will be focused and will have a scorecard." Scott handed over to Brown the sample report the Infoman had given him. "This is the way I want the reports to look," he said.

Brown looked at the sample report. There was a long moment of silence. He was not impressed. "This is not a big deal," he thought. He was surprised Scott was asking for such a report. Brown felt it would be a complete waste of time.

Scott noticed Brown's reaction and his reluctance to do what he was being asked.

"What's bothering you?" he asked.

"The information you are asking for is already available in reports we receive from several sources. It's all there. We've got enough trouble handling the information we get and now you want us to duplicate the work. We're already working hard doing our best for the company."

Brown continued, "We do a lot of fire fighting every day to keep things going. Instead of recognizing our hard work, you are telling me to waste my people's time preparing a report."

"I appreciate the efforts your people are expending," replied Scott, "but that doesn't mean I have to accept the outcomes. Just because you are working hard doesn't mean you are doing the right things.

*

*It's More Important
To Be Doing
The Right
Things*

*Than To Be
Doing Things Right.*

*

"That's why I want you to go through this experience of defining the Critical Success Factors for yourselves," Scott added.

"Your people will have to struggle to weed out what's important and what's unimportant. By the time you are finished, managers will have a list of the 'right things' to work hard on. This will help turn the company around."

It was difficult for Brown to see Scott's point of view. It went against his grain. He was upset. Yet he wanted to be part of the team and had a sincere interest in the success of the company. He told Scott he'd do what he could.

Scott had expected Brown to be much more enthusiastic. Brown's reactions disturbed Scott. "This type of attitude may well be a cultural norm at Xcorp and could be a clue to Xcorp's malaise," thought Scott.

Brown left Scott's office and walked directly to the office of his close friend, the vice-president in charge of planning. "The new CEO is a nut," he said as he entered the office. "He thinks we're sitting around with nothing to do. He doesn't realize I am working on important projects and can't afford the luxury of reformatting reports."

The vice-president of planning was a diplomatic fellow. "Scott probably has a good reason for what he is asking, but if you don't like it, all you have to do is nothing; let it stay in the backlog of work."

"That'll do the trick all right," replied Brown sarcastically. "It'll get me fired."

"No, it won't," said the VP for planning. "If you tell him you are working on it and drag your feet for a while, chances are Scott will forget about it, and your problem will blow away."

"Drag my feet! Some advice!" thought Brown, disappointed in his colleague's response. He walked to his own office and sat in his chair. He didn't even notice his secretary's hello.

It was 3:00 P.M. Brown glanced at his schedule for the rest of the afternoon. He had looked forward to attending two meetings: "Shop Floor Automation" and "Integrated Manufacturing Computer System." He didn't feel like attending either meeting. They seemed irrelevant.

Brown called his secretary. "I'm not attending any meetings this afternoon. The presentations can start without me." He felt that with Scott's new demand, he would be asked to abandon major projects in which he had invested considerable time and energy. He was disoriented.

Brown was staring at the wall when suddenly there was a knock at the door. It was his secretary. "I'm leaving, and I wonder if there is anything I can do," she said. Brown looked at his watch. It was five o'clock. "No, thank you," he replied. "Good-bye."

Brown decided he might as well go home. He got up and left his office. He carried his bad mood home, walking slowly and without a smile on his face. His wife knew something had happened. She could tell Brown's mood by the way he entered the house. This was not the usual robust person she knew. She wanted to ask him what was wrong, but decided to wait until after dinner when the children were in bed.

That evening the Brown family had the quietest dinner they had had for a long time. Every effort to get conversation going failed. After dinner, Tom Brown sat in his recliner, picked up the newspaper, and stared at it.

"Honey, why are you looking at the job section?" asked Brown's wife, Elaine. "Did you get fired?"

"No, but if things get difficult at Xcorp and if I can't get along with Scott, I may have to start looking around," he replied.

"What are you talking about?" she exclaimed. "You've been particularly excited about your job in the last year. What happened today?"

"The new CEO is an idiot, and he dislikes me."

"Now, calm down, he can't be an idiot if he is running Xcorp, and I can't imagine anyone not liking you. Tell me what really happened. Don't give me your opinions, just give me the facts."

"The CEO was on my back today. He spent a good part of the afternoon interrogating me about my Critical Success Factors for production."

"What is he asking you to do?" asked Elaine.

"To spend our time defining Critical Success Factors and goals so each manager can look at one piece of paper rather than at a whole lot of different reports," replied Tom.

"What's wrong with that?" asked Elaine.

"It's crazy, that's what's wrong with it! It's a waste of time and money. If he wants a One Page Report, let him construct one for himself but leave me alone. Besides, I have enough trouble communicating with our people. Can you imagine getting managers to prepare new reports? We'll be spending all of our time talking. I'm not going to do it. I know what's best for the company. It's not what Scott is asking." Tom kept talking and repeating himself.

Elaine was getting angry with her husband. She tried several times to say something, but Tom wouldn't give her a chance.

She suddenly got up, took a pile of newspapers and slammed it on the table. "Will you stop acting like a child and listen to me? You're being stubborn. You don't want to admit that you may be wrong. Why don't you look at it from his point of view?"

She continued, "Ask yourself, 'Why does this guy want me to develop One Page Reports?' There might be some logical reason besides thinking he is crazy."

Tom had never seen his wife so assertive. He liked it, but didn't admit it and kept quiet.

Elaine softened her voice, "Honey, do you remember last Friday evening's dinner at the neighbors'?"

"How could I forget that awful dinner?" replied Tom.

"The steak they served us was the most expensive cut of meat. Steak is your favorite food, isn't it? They had fried it in a mushroom and butter sauce, and it was overcooked. You like your steak medium broiled with no butter and no sauce."

"That's right."

"So you didn't eat the steak they served, and that didn't make them feel very good."

"What does this have to do with my boss?" asked Tom.

"Everything," replied Elaine. "The efforts you are putting in for your CEO are like the well-done steak."

She continued, "Don't you see? He likes his steak cooked a different way. Why not find out how he likes his steak cooked and cook it for him that way? And that should be easy because the man is telling you the way he wants his company organized."

Elaine then paused for a few minutes and said, "Besides, honey, don't forget the golden rule: He who has the gold makes the rule."

Tom kept quiet. "I hope I haven't been talking to the wall," said Elaine as she left the room.

Tom understood his wife's point. He realized that he couldn't take on both his wife and his boss. He began to try to see things from Scott's point of view. He thought for a long time and finally decided he would have to give One Page Management a try.

The next day Brown met with his direct subordinates and discussed the assignment he had been given by Scott. He asked them to get together to construct their One Page Reports. His subordinates were pleased to be involved. Brown's team met on two consecutive Saturdays in Brown's conference room.

Brown's subordinates followed the Infoman's Four Simple Steps. Each person identified his important relationships, and defined success areas and success factors from the viewpoints of these relationships.

On the second Saturday, Brown's team had brought all the reports they were currently receiving. They stacked them up for fun, and it measured six feet high. The prospects of summarizing all the management information on one page intrigued them. They went through the reports and extracted the status of the Critical Success Factors they had defined. When they had finished, each had a Focus Report similar to the one the Infoman had shown Scott.

Brown noticed how the Focus Report displayed all of the managers' performance areas on the same document. This exercise had focused the managers' attention on what was important. He saw on his subordinates' Focus Reports Critical Success Factors he hadn't noticed before, and he realized that the status of many was a lot worse than he had realized. The experience changed Brown's attitude. "Maybe there is something to this One Page Management after all," he thought.

On Monday, while Brown was thinking over the meeting with his subordinates, he realized that he had not defined his own One Page Report.

He asked his secretary to prepare his Focus Report by combining the Focus Reports of his subordinates. By the end of the day his secretary had finished the task, and Brown had a typed copy of a Focus Report that looked similar to the one Scott had shown him, but it was two and a half pages.

"Well," thought Brown, "two and a half pages isn't too bad for someone with my degree of responsibility."

Brown was now happy that Scott had asked him to construct these reports, although it was difficult for him to admit it to himself. It had given him and his people the opportunity to think about some major issues they had never taken time to address. He was proud that he had a document to show for his people's time and effort.

Brown called Scott for an appointment to discuss One Page Management. Brown's interest surprised Scott. He had already made plans to start the program in the sales area because of Brown's initial response.

"I have my report ready," declared Brown. "One Page Management is not a bad program. But of course the proof of the pudding is yet to come."

Scott was curious to see what had caused Brown's change in attitude. He wanted to see Brown's report but felt that the Infoman should be present to comment on it. He asked his secretary to set up a meeting for him with the Infoman and Brown.

"But I don't have the Infoman's phone number," replied the secretary.

"That's frustrating," sighed Scott. "We'll have to schedule it when he calls."

When she returned to her desk, the phone was ringing. It was the Infoman. She laughed.

"I thought you might be calling. Mr. Scott would like to arrange a meeting with you and Mr. Brown."

The meeting was arranged for Thursday morning.

THURSDAY morning Brown entered Scott's office feeling pleased with himself but leery about the Infoman's presence at the meeting. Scott introduced them. The Infoman greeted Brown warmly, and Brown responded with a cool nod. He wished he were alone with Scott.

Ignoring the Infoman, Brown looked at Scott and said, "You gave me some good ideas."

"What do you mean?" asked the CEO.

"I'm talking about the Focus Report," replied Brown.

Brown appeared to mean what he said. He continued, "The pieces of this report that existed before were not well defined or consistent. When we put them together to construct the One Page Report, we were surprised at the impact it had on all of us."

Brown felt that he now understood One Page Management, that he knew why the One Page Report was necessary, how it was constructed, and how it could be used.

"Was it hard work?" asked Scott.

"Nothing to it," said Brown. "It was easy. Compared to other management programs, there were no old habits to change, no behaviors to modify. It was a cinch."

Scott smiled and replied, "I am glad you found it easy. My report was not so easy to construct. Tell me about your experience."

"We had a lot of fun defining our Critical Success Factors," said Brown. "It helped us a lot more than I thought it would. And after we finished, we wondered why we hadn't done it before."

"When you say 'we,' whom are you referring to?" asked the Infoman.

"Myself and my direct subordinates. We had a couple of brainstorming sessions, and we developed our Focus Reports."

"I bet your people enjoyed being involved," said the Infoman.

"They sure did," responded Brown, as he opened his briefcase and took out his two and a half page report.

The Infoman examined Brown's report for a while. He then looked up and said, "You've put a lot of effort into this report, and I commend you for it. However, there are a couple of things I need to point out. Most people have the same problems when they first begin One Page Management. So please don't take my comments as a criticism of your work."

Brown nodded his head as he listened for the Infoman's comments.

"First of all, why is your report more than one page?"

Brown was tempted to ignore the Infoman and pretend he didn't hear the question, but he realized how intently Scott was listening. "Well, it seemed like I just couldn't leave out my direct subordinates' Critical Success Factors on my report," he replied.

"How many direct subordinates do you have?" asked the Infoman.

"Three," answered Brown.

"What would you do if you had ten people reporting to you directly? Would you repeat all their Critical Success Factors on your report and end up with ten pages?" asked the Infoman.

"I guess I would," replied Brown.

The Infoman said, "In that case, I haven't clearly communicated the real benefits of One Page Management in terms of managing information."

Brown didn't quite expect this kind of response when he thought he had mastered One Page Management.

"What do you mean?" Brown asked the Infoman.

The Infoman smiled and said, "The Critical Success Factors on each person's report should be unique to that person. Your Focus Report must have different Critical Success Factors. It shouldn't be just a repetition of your subordinates' factors."

"But I'm their manager, so how can my Critical Success Factors be separate from theirs?" asked Brown.

"Let me give you an example," said the Infoman. "If your subordinates' Critical Success Factors include units of goods shipped, yours could be inventory turnover or product profitability. If they are concerned with the number of units produced, your Critical Success Factor should deal with how these units meet customer needs."

That sounded reasonable to Brown, who loved to hear manufacturing terms. He realized that the Infoman knew something about manufacturing operations and began to take him seriously.

"The problem is," said Brown, "that it is impossible to define unique Critical Success Factors for me that do not also apply to my direct subordinates."

The Infoman looked at Brown with an understanding expression on his face. He smiled and asked, "Do you think your job is necessary?"

Brown was on the spot. He knew the Infoman was asking the question to illustrate a point. Nevertheless, such a question in front of his boss made him uneasy.

Scott answered the question for Brown. "Of course Brown's job is necessary," he said.

The Infoman continued, "If it is impossible to define unique Critical Success Factors for a manager beyond what is defined for his subordinates, that is a clear sign that the manager's job is not necessary.

"Many managers simply watch the lower ranks do their work. And they do their watching through endless meetings.

"I know your job is necessary," said the Infoman to Brown, "so there must be a way of defining those unique Critical Success Factors for you."

Brown paused for a moment. "I have to coordinate all manufacturing activities from scheduling to shipment."

"There you are," said the Infoman. "Your Critical Success Factors must be defined to reflect your success in your coordination effort. Additionally, at your level, you are probably in charge of implementing plans for product enhancement, the development of new products, and the implementation of new technologies that would reduce the cost of production and improve the quality of your products. Your Critical Success Factors should reflect your success in these sorts of implementation efforts too."

This made Brown more comfortable. He took a deep breath. He was beginning to see what the Infoman was saying. He had never thought about his job in this way.

"It requires a lot of creativity to come up with unique factors for yourself. You must refer to the Four Simple Steps," said the Infoman.

"Your Critical Success Factors should be related to overall productivity and effectiveness. There is nothing wrong, of course, with including totals and averages of your subordinates' Critical Success Factors on your report, but you must realize that if you concentrate solely on those kinds of Critical Success Factors, you'll weaken the accountability system."

Brown began to appreciate the Infoman. "Would you please have another look at my report," he said, now feeling more relaxed, "and tell me if I have at least set my goals correctly?"

The Infoman looked at Brown's report again. His current status in some cases was better than the Outstanding Goal Level. The Infoman asked, "Why is it that you have set your outstanding goals lower than your current status for some of these Critical Success Factors?"

"THOSE goals are the industrial engineering standards," suggested Brown.

"Do you get a sense of accomplishment when you beat those standards?" asked the Infoman.

"Not at all," replied Brown. "It's so easy."

"Then those standards are not high enough. I know you want to keep improving. Therefore, you have to pick Satisfactory Goal Levels that are higher than your current status and achievable in a short term. And your Outstanding Goal Level should be tough enough to ensure a high standard of excellence."

"Do you suggest altering our standards?"

"I don't see why not," said the Infoman. "They are not sacred. They have been determined by a group of people who came, measured the job, and picked the numbers. If you have new machinery, then those standards are out-of-date. If you are already beating the standards, then select higher goals."

The Infoman took another look at the report and said, "I don't know your job, so I can't determine if these Success Factors adequately define your success, but I must say, this is a good beginning."

The Infoman suggested that Brown go back and fix his Focus Report before getting further input. He got up, shook hands with Scott and Brown, and left.

Brown left Scott's office full of ideas. He decided he would fix his Focus Report right away before the Infoman's input faded. He went to his office, cleared his conference table, and sat down with a pad of paper and his two and a half page report.

He started modifying the report by taking out, one by one, the Critical Success Factors that applied to his direct subordinates. When he had finished that task, he ended up with a blank page.

Brown then struggled to pinpoint unique Critical Success Factors for himself. He suddenly blushed as he recalled his conversation with Scott when Scott had asked him to enumerate his Critical Success Factors. He had said that the list would fill two hundred pages. Now he was having trouble coming up with one entry. He was discouraged and about ready to give up.

Suddenly Brown remembered a statement of the Infoman's that kept him on task. "If you can't define unique Critical Success Factors for your job, then maybe the job isn't necessary." He got up, poured himself some coffee, and returned to his office full of energy and determination.

Brown wrote down what he considered to be his major contribution to the company. He felt that in addition to being in charge of ongoing production, he was also responsible for the future health of the company. The automation of the manufacturing process, the scrap-reduction program, and productivity improvement were the major projects he was involved in.

His responsibilities for the ongoing operation of Xcorp manufacturing required his attention to the quality and on-time delivery of Xcorp products, the turnover of inventories, the control of waste, and the overall efficiency of Xcorp plants.

He thought and thought about each of these areas and how he could define Critical Success Factors. He used the Four Simple Steps the Infoman had given to Scott. Over the next several days, applying the four steps forced him to talk to a lot of people in sales, finance, production planning, research and development. He got several good ideas from these conversations and found valuable information. For example, the sales area could provide him with information on customer complaints and rejects, product enhancement, and competitive products. Accounting records gave him inventory adjustments and costs associated with inventory growth.

Brown's search made him more aware of the interrelationship of the various functions within the company. The more involved Brown became in the project, the more he saw the value of what Scott wanted him to do.

In two weeks Brown's report was ready. He had shown his report to his close friend, the VP of planning, and based on his suggestion, Brown had grouped his Critical Success Factors into two major categories. He labeled the first category OPERATIONS and named the second category PROJECTS.

Brown entered unique Critical Success Factors dealing with the ongoing operation of his plants. These included the movement of inventories, on-time shipment to the customer, overall returns from the customer, overall efficiency, and overall labor turnover.

The second category was the challenging one. Brown listed several projects that dealt with the future operations of Xcorp. He felt this would get Scott's attention. These projects included manu-facturing automation, productivity improvement, and product enhancement. Brown added the special austerity-budget cost-cutting project to this category.

Brown was proud of the report he had defined. He knew that the attention he was going to give to his newly defined Critical Success Factors would have a major impact on the company's profitability. He contacted Scott's secretary to arrange a meeting with Scott and the Infoman.

The three men were back together within three weeks of the Infoman's last visit. Brown was more confident and self-assured. He knew his job was necessary.

"How did it go?" the Infoman asked Brown.

"Great" was Brown's reply. "I have a One Page Report with unique Critical Success Factors relevant to me." He handed over copies of his report to Scott and the Infoman.

SUCCESS DEFINED FOR TOM BROWN
Week Ending February 24

Critical Success Factors	Status	Minimum Level	Satisfactory Goal Level	Outstanding Goal Level	Trend

CATEGORY 1—OPERATIONS

Critical Success Factors	Status	Minimum Level	Satisfactory Goal Level	Outstanding Goal Level	Trend
Complaints per 1,000 Pounds	12	15	10	5	B
Money Lost Sales to Manufacturing (× 1,000)	500	800	300	50	B
% Rejeccts Due to Raw Materials	50	60	30	15	B
% Overall First Quality	92	94	97	99	B
% Overall Efficiency	98.5	95	98	100	G
% Shipments Just-in-Time	11	20	30	40	G
% Aged Inventory over 60 days	80	30	25	10	B

CATEGORY 2—PROJECTS

Critical Success Factors	Status	Minimum Level	Satisfactory Goal Level	Outstanding Goal Level	Trend
% Variance Against the Austerity Budget	20	10	5	0	—
Automation Project Phase I	Done	May 1	April 15	April 1	—
Productivity Program Phase II	Phase I	August 1	July 1	June 15	—

The Infoman examined Brown's report. He was pleased and surprised at Brown's creativity. He liked the two categories Brown had used. He looked at Brown with a smile and said, "Brown, you've done a fantastic job. This is great! Now you have an exceptional tool for improving performance."

Scott also joined the Infoman in praising Brown. The praise from the Infoman and Scott made Brown feel good.

"I like the way you have considered the two broad categories of Operations and Projects," said the Infoman.

"People at the lower levels of the management pyramid should be concerned with running present operations effectively. Their Critical Success Factors are mainly related to the ongoing operations of the company.

"As you move up the organization, you should become more future-oriented. The amount of time you spend on keeping the present operations going should decrease, while your efforts at building a better future should increase."

"What an exciting idea!" commented Scott. "Getting our upper-level managers to become future oriented is a change that is badly needed here."

While Scott was thinking about the Infoman's explanation, Brown was wondering how he could live with only a One Page Report with unique Critical Succcess Factors. He put the question to the Infoman.

"Since my Focus Report does not repeat my subordinates' Critical Success Factors, and if it is the only report I look at, then how do I know how they're doing?"

The Infoman smiled. "Good question," he said. "The Focus Report is not the only report you look at. The Second and Third One Page Reports will help you out. The One Page Reports of your managers get linked together through the third report. With that report you'll know how your people are doing. Before we look at that report though, let's look at the Second One Page Report.

"The Second One Page Report is called the FEEDBACK REPORT. It helps you watch your progress on your way to success."

"How does it do that?"

"**R**EMEMBER our discussion about success," said the Infoman. "First you defined success; then you determined how you'd know when you'd made it. Well, watching your progress simply means examining the status for each Critical Success Factor to see if you've made your Satisfactory Goal Level. If you have, you should celebrate. If you haven't, you should think of adjusting your strategy and game plan, and staying on course.

"That's what I mean by watching your progress. Now let's construct the Feedback Report to help us do the watching."

The Infoman asked Scott for the latest version of his Focus Report. He examined that report, then took a sheet of paper, copied some information from Scott's report onto this sheet and showed it to Scott.

WATCHING PROGRESS TOWARD SUCCESS FOR BRIAN SCOTT
Week Ending February 24

You've Made Your Goal—Congratulations

Critical Success Factors	Status	Satisfactory Goal
Reorganization Plan	Ahead	March 30
Inventory Turnover per Month	5	5

You Have Problems—Think Smarter

Critical Success Factors	Status	Minimum Goal
Market Share	9.9%	12%

"You can see at a glance where your strengths and weaknesses are," said the Infoman. "Look, you've achieved your Satisfatory Goal Levels on the Reorganization Project and Inventory Turnover. That's good news. The bad news is that your Market Share is behind your Minimum Level. You've got to be more creative to improve this."

The Infoman turned to Brown and suggested, "Try constructing the Feedback Report for yourself based on your Focus Report."

Brown took a sheet of paper and drew a horizontal line across the middle of the page. He wrote the title "You've Made Your Goal—Congratulations" on the upper part and "You Have Problems—Think Smarter" on the lower part.

Brown then examined against the Satisfactory Goal Level each Critical Success Factor on his Focus Report. If his status was better than this goal level, he copied that critical Success Factor and its status onto the upper part of the page.

"Let's call these POSITIVE results," said the Infoman.

Brown then looked at each of his Critical Success Factors again. This time he evaluated his status against the Minimum Level. If his status was worse than the Minimum Level, he copied that Critical Success Factor and its status onto the lower part of the paper.

"Let's call these NEGATIVE results," said the Infoman.

When Brown was finished, the sheet looked like this:

WATCHING PROGRESS TOWARD SUCCESS
FOR TOM BROWN
Week Ending February 24

You've Made Your Goal—Congratulations

Critical Success Factor	Status	Satisfactory Goal
% Overall Efficiency	98.5	98
Automation Project		
Phase I	Ahead	April 15

You Have Problems—Think Smarter

Critical Success Factors	Status	Minimum Level
% Overall First Quality	92	94
% Shipments Just-in-Time	11	20
% Variance Austerity Budget	20	10

Brown had two entries in the upper part and three in the lower part of the page.

The Infoman and Scott were watching Brown go through this exercise, which took a few minutes.

"Great! Look what a good job you have done," commented the Infoman. "You have two positives. Two of your Critical Success Factors have been above your Satisfactory Goal Level. That should make you feel good."

"I'll bet you didn't know before going through this exercise that you had these positives, even though you had all of the information in front of you."

"I must admit I hadn't taken time to look at what I was doing right," said Brown.

The Infoman continued, "Here you're looking at summary information. Don't you think this summary is fun to look at?"

"It depends on what the bad news is," replied Brown with a chuckle.

"Whatever it is, it's better to know it right away," said the Infoman, "so that you can fix it.

"I think you're going to like the Feedback Report so much that you'll wonder how you ever managed without it. You'll probably look at this even before you examine your Focus Report."

Brown looked puzzled again and said, "But the Critical Success Factors that were neither positive nor negative don't appear on this report."

"Don't worry about those," replied the Infoman. "Assuming your goals are set properly, the ones that are neither positive nor negative are within the acceptable range of achievement."

"I don't understand," said Brown.

The Infoman took his pad and drew another square, this time with the Minimum and Satisfactory Goal lines slanting upward. He then put a hypothetical graph inside the square and showed it to Brown and Scott. "The performance in the middle area is within your defined acceptable bounds," he stated.

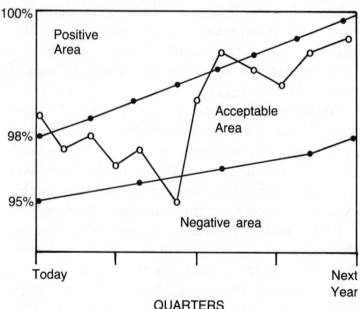

OVERALL EFFICIENCY

Scott nodded his head. He agreed with the Infoman. "That's an interesting way of doing Management by Exception," he said.

The Infoman laughed. "Never thought of it that way—you're right. Especially if managers remember not to dwell solely on the negative exceptions. The power of One Page Management comes from reinforcing the positive exceptions."

"So this is the Second One Page Report," stated Scott.

"Not quite. We need to add a couple of features to it before we have the report I have been referring to."

"Let's look at one of your positives, Overall Efficiency," said the Infoman turning to Brown. "The fact that your latest status was better than your Satisfactory Goal Level is great news. But your latest status doesn't tell you if you have everything in place to sustain that good result. You need your TRACK RECORD on this Critical Success Factor.

"I suggest," he continued, "that you need two pieces of information that will show you your track record. You need to know how many periods or weeks in a row your performance has been positive. And you need to look at a historical graph of your status to discover if there is a pattern indicating whether or not you're moving toward your goal. You see, on the road to success you have to know if you are headed in the right direction. If you are, I'd say your trend is 'G' for good. Otherwise, your trend will be 'B' for bad."

The Infoman then discussed the track record of Brown's Critical Success Factors with him, added the two pieces of information to the sheet of paper he had prepared, and showed it to Scott and Brown.

WATCHING PROGRESS TOWARD SUCCESS FOR TOM BROWN
Week Ending February 24

You've Made Your Goal—Congratulations

Critical Success Factors	Status	Satisfactory Goal Level	Periods in a Row	Trend
% Overall Efficiency	98.5	98	3	G
Automation Project Phase I	Ahead	April 15	—	—

You Have Problems—Think Smarter

% Overall First Quality	92	94	5	B
% Shipments Just-in-Time	11	20	3	G
% Variance Austery Budget	20	10	1	—

"This is too good to be true," exclaimed Brown, who realized how this report would help him focus on critical areas needing attention.

"You see," explained the Infoman, "looking at this sheet, you know your strengths and weaknesses, and the direction you're heading in.

"How can I have a problem in percent shipment just-in-time if the trend is good?" asked Brown.

"Good question," replied the Infoman. "Although you're making progress, your performance is still worse than the Minimum Level."

The Infoman then turned to Scott and said, "Now I've told you everything you need to know to use the Focus Report and the Feedback Report. All of your people from the hourly employee to your level can start using both reports in the format I've described beginning tomorrow. I think you have everything you need to start."

"Do you suggest we start without the Third One Page Report?" asked Scott.

"Definitely," was the Infoman's answer. "Later, when your managers become used to managing with the information contained in their Focus and Feedback Reports, you can link your people's Feedback Reports together. When you do that, the Focus Report will gain another column. I'll discuss this column later."

The Infoman got up, said good-bye to Scott and Brown, and wished them well in implementing One Page Management.

SCOTT was eager to get Xcorp started on One Page Management. He decided that the best strategy was to develop a manual that clearly explained the development and use of the first two One Page Reports. The only person who had been exposed to One Page Management so far was Brown. Scott gave Brown all the notes he had taken during his conversations with the Infoman and asked him to put them together into a manual. Scott asked Gail Locke to edit the manual. That task would enable her to become thoroughly conversant with the concepts. He wanted her to develop a training and coaching program for implementing One Page Management.

One month later the manual and the training materials were ready. They were written in a clear and simple style, and they were fun to read. Scott gave copies to all managers in the organization as the first step to implementing One Page Management.

Xcorp managers read and reread the manuals at their own pace and made notes in the margins of the pages. This helped them understand the principles described. It helped them learn how to use information as a means to success. They didn't feel threatened because they saw the value of the reports, and they became aware of the overall direction of the corporation.

The participation in the training and coaching program was poor at first, but improved rapidly. The visible success of managers who had taken the course encouraged others to enroll.

Xcorp's Kansas wire-manufacturing plant had the highest percent of participation. Arnold Turner, a newly promoted department manager at that plant, became the champion of the program there. Turner, a machine operator for ten years, had recently made a turnaround in his performance, and this was mainly responsible for his promotion. He attributed his success to goal setting and performance tracking. He liked the way the One Page Reports helped him stay focused. He was pleased that Scott had initiated the program.

In four months Scott's scheme was producing results. Sixty percent of Xcorp management had been trained and coached. Focus and Feedback Reports had been produced at each level of management and were being updated by managers each week.

Scott had been involved throughout the process. His level of interest had increased continuously. He reviewed many of the Focus Reports, asked questions, and learned much about the company.

One day it suddenly occurred to Scott that the information problem as he had first defined it was already solved. Through the process of definition of managers' Critical Success Factors and viewing their status, he had answered his original questions about the company.

The One Page Management practices that were evolving went way beyond Scott's original view of the problem. He recalled the Infoman and his advice. He had not seen the Infoman for several months.

While Scott was occupied with these thoughts, the phone rang. Scott's secretary informed him that the Infoman was on the line.

"Put him on," said Scott.

"How is it going?"

"Great! I was just thinking about you."

"I am glad you haven't forgotten me," said the Infoman. "Are you ready for my next visit?"

"We sure are. The majority of our managers have defined their Critical Success Factors and goals. They are updating their Focus Reports weekly."

"How long have they been doing One Page Management?"

"A couple of months," replied Scott.

"I can see you at nine A.M. on Thursday."

Scott confirmed the date.

PART III

*Linking the
One Page Reports*

IT was Thursday morning. Turner was meeting with his plant manager in Kansas. He was receiving praise for the excellent performance of his department. During his previous year as department manager, he had saved the company close to a million dollars through increased efficiency, decrease in off-quality production, and substantial reduction of scrap. The plant manager was pleased. He gave Turner a 30 percent increase in salary. Turner was happy.

At the same time Turner was receiving a raise in Kansas, Scott was in his office getting ready for the Infoman's visit. He had risen early and left for his office shortly after seven. Now it was only 8:00 A.M. and he was standing by the window looking out at the nearby park.

Scott reflected on what he had learned from the Infoman. Each individual component of One Page Management seemed to be something he already knew, but he had never thought about combining it in this way. It was the way of looking at success and striving for excellence that was so great. He thought for a few minutes and realized that the power of One Page Management was the way the Feedback Report helped managers see at one glance what deserved to get their attention. Yet what was equally exciting was the effect these reports had on people.

Scott's phone rang and interrupted his train of thought. His secretary informed him that the Infoman was ready to see him.

"How has it been going since our last meeting?" the Infoman asked Scott.

"Beyond my expectations," replied Scott. "Frankly," he said, "I now realize that there is so much to learn about information. Every time we use the One Page Reports, we see new benefits."

Scott was anxious to tell the Infoman about the experience his people had had with One Page Management.

"Let me tell you how this approach has changed the life of one of Brown's people," began Scott. "Lucy Lake was one of our quality-assurance people whom Brown recently promoted to a plant manager. The transformation of this young woman is phenomenal."

"Tell me the story," requested the Infoman.

"I am told that one year ago, Lake was an average quality-control department head. She could not solve major quality problems in her plant. Since One Page Management, however, quality has been improving in her area. Her plant now ranks number one in quality as measured by the extent of returned goods from the customer.

"One Page Management helped her gain control over her performance at work. She loved the way the Feedback Report kept her attention on the positive and the negative results. She had fun devising clever ways of solving problems highlighted in that report. Her plans were usually effective, and when they helped her hit a positive, she felt good. We saw her smiling a lot."

Scott continued, "Lake told Brown that one day she decided she wanted to improve her personal life too. Since One Page Management had put her in control of her performance at work, she felt the same principles could help her with her personal goals. For a start, she didn't want to be overweight anymore.

"Lake defined a Focus Report for herself that included Critical Success Factors on health, diet, exercise, and financial affairs. She devised a way of recording information on each factor in a notebook. On a weekly basis she constructed her Focus Report and her Feedback Report.

"Lake reviewed her progress weekly by looking at the positives and the negatives. The transformation was phenomenal. She told Brown that within three months she had reached her Satisfactory Goal Level in all the areas, and had no negatives. She tightened her goals and kept on improving. Brown promoted her a month ago, and she already is doing her new job better than the previous plant manager."

The Infoman was pleased to hear Lake's success story. It was a natural lead-in to the next subject he wanted to discuss. He looked at Scott and said, "How did you find out about Lake?"

"We were monitoring the One Page Management program, and Brown happened to be in a meeting where Lake's name was mentioned," replied Scott.

"With the Third One Page Report," said the Infoman, "you will have firsthand knowledge of the excellent performers like Lucy Lake every time."

"How?" asked Scott.

The Infoman smiled. "By linking the One Page Reports of your managers together."

"That sounds like a challenging idea," responded Scott.

The Infoman began to talk about the linkage of the reports. "You recall that while your Focus and Feedback Reports give you relevant information about your own Critical Success Factors, they don't tell you what's going on below you."

"That's true," commented Scott.

"Wouldn't you like to know about the performance of your subordinates and people below your subordinates?"

"I sure would," stated Scott.

"How do you suppose this can be done?"

"I could receive a copy of my subordinates' Focus Reports," answered Scott.

"That's certainly a solution. However, with the name Infoman, I could not promote it. It would cause you information overload."

"Then I could receive a copy of my subordinates' Feedback Reports," commented Scott.

"That's definitely better. It would make you aware of the status of all the Critical Success Factors of your people that were positive or negative. But that would also cause you information overload.

"Imagine," continued the Infoman, "having one piece of paper that gives you all the good news and bad news about the work of people you directly manage."

"That would be wonderful!" commented Scott.

"Furthermore, imagine the same sheet of paper containing the best of all the good news on your people's achievements coming from several layers below you."

"That would be great!" exclaimed Scott.

"Similarly, what if the same sheet of paper could give you the worst of all the bad news from lower levels, problems that probably deserve your attention. Moreover, suppose you were assured that what you see on this piece of paper is what there is—in other words, that nothing has fallen through the cracks."

Scott was sitting at the edge of his chair. "Is this possible?" he asked.

"Indeed" was the Infoman's answer. "This is what happens when you link the Feedback Reports via the Third One Page Report, the MANAGEMENT REPORT."

Scott was intrigued. He was curious to discover how the linkage was done.

The Infoman smiled. "Here's how it works. Let's suppose you had three people directly reporting to you. Then all the positive and negative exceptions that appear on these direct subordinates' Feedback Reports are exactly the information you would see on the RIGHT-HAND SIDE of your MANAGEMENT REPORT, positives on the top and negatives on the bottom of the sheet."

"This is equivalent to sending me my direct subordinates' Feedback Reports," commented Scott.

"Yes, it is," said the Infoman, "except that with the Management Report you are dealing with summarized information on One Page."

Scott's face showed a great degree of satisfaction. He smiled. "What goes into the LEFT-HAND SIDE of the Management Report?" he asked.

"Now into the most exciting and unique feature of One Page Management," responded the Infoman.

The Infoman got up, went to a white board, took a Magic Marker, and drew a vertical line. He then drew a picture of a manager at the top of the board followed underneath by pictures of five managers, each below the other, representing several layers of management.

"Suppose these people have their Focus and Feedback Reports. They know their progress on all their Critical Success Factors.

"Now, some of the positives these managers have accomplished through working hard and smart are truly exceptional. When you link the One Page Reports together via the Management Report, then you will be able to notice people like Lucy Lake on the left-hand side of your Management Report."

"I wonder why it's always been so difficult to notice the great performers in the company," said Scott with a sigh.

"I can explain why," said the Infoman. "But let me first ask you a question. If a person at the bottom on this board does a really good job, who knows about it under Xcorp's present system?"

"The person above him, his boss."

"If it is an extremely good job, who notices that?" asked the Infoman.

"The same person," responded Scott.

"Who gets the credit for that good performance? The person who did it or his boss?"

"Unfortunately, usually his boss," responded Scott.

"Now, that's not fair," said the Infoman. "It encourages managers to delay promoting excellent performers as long as they can; and often, by the time the promotion comes, that performer is too old or too tired."

Scott agreed with the Infoman. "When a manager has good performers who make him look good and get all the credit, he is tempted to keep them reporting to him as long as possible. It's called job security," said Scott.

"I'm sad to say," continued the Infoman with a sigh, "that this is the way it is in many companies. I think that things need to change. To me, the most unique and exciting aspect of One Page Management is this feature."

Scott was equally excited about this concept. "The way your system makes performance transparent up the line will allow each individual to receive credit for his own excellent performance, while his boss will receive credit for managing him right."

"Exactly," exclaimed the Infoman. "If a person's performance is truly exceptional, I don't see why it should not be reported all the way up the line to you, so he can get the credit. Wouldn't you like to know about that excellent performer?"

"I sure would. I like to get to know my people."

The Infoman took a red Magic Marker and drew an arrow starting from the individual at the lowest level on the white board all the way to the top manager. "You've got to notice people many levels removed from you."

"What about reporting the negatives up the line?" asked Scott.

"The same principle holds for the negatives."

"But don't too many levels of management then get involved in a problem the manager's immediate boss should handle?"

"They don't," replied the Infoman, "because you decide at what point you want problems to be reported up the line. You can allow the individual and his boss ample time to solve the problem.

"For example, you can decide that any Critical Success Factor that has been positive or negative for more than four periods in a row will be reported up the line two levels above the manager responsible for that factor. It could be reported to three levels above if it continues to be positive or negative for more than eight weeks in a row.

"Therefore, what appears on the upper left side of your Management Report is what has been positive or negative long enough to require your attention based on the rules we've just discussed.

"When the reports are linked, the Feedback Report gains an additional column that tells the recipient which good news or bad news has been reported to upper levels."

"I agree, it'll be motivating for my people to know I am aware of their positives," said Scott.

"You have just described the power of One Page Management," said the Infoman. "Those super performers get motivated by looking at their Feedback Reports."

The Infoman drew a square on a sheet of paper and divided it into four zones. He labeled each zone and suggested that what he had just been talking about would easily fit into these zones. "This is the structure of the Management Report."

THE THIRD ONE PAGE REPORT
MANAGEMENT REPORT

Indirect Subordinates
Several Levels Below

Direct Subordinates
One Level Below

Zone 1: Positive	**Zone 2:** Positive
Highlights of Excellent Performance of Managers Several Levels Below	Highlights and Details of Good Performance of Direct Subordinates
Zone 3: Negative	**Zone 4:** Negative
Highlights of Chronic Performance Problems from Several Levels Below	Highlights and Details of Performance Problems of Direct Subordinates

Scott picked up the Management Report structure the Infoman was showing him and looked at it for a few minutes. "If I look only at this report, what would I be missing about the performance of my people?" Scott asked.

"Nothing significant," said the Infoman with a smile. "This report is complete if two conditions are satisfied. The first condition is that each of your managers has accurately defined all his major Critical Success Factors, and the second condition is that each manager's goals are set properly. Then this report would pick up every 'out of range' condition from below, positive or negative, that deserves your attention.

"Assuming these conditions are satisfied," promised the Infoman, "you can rest assured when reading this report that nothing has fallen through the cracks."

That seemed logical. However, satisfying the two conditions was not easy to do, thought Scott. "Isn't it difficult to ensure that your two conditions are satisfied?" he asked.

"I didn't say it was easy, but I can say with certainty that it is essential if you want to continue to be successful."

Scott knew that he had to take care of the two conditions.

The Infoman picked up the Management Report sample. He paused and said, "The information on this report will enable managers to provide more effective leadership through better communication with their people. This report gives substance to the concept of 'management by walking around' because it provides managers with something positive and specific to talk about while meeting people."

"For example," he continued, "you can communicate praise on a specific positive performance to subordinates in the elevator right in front of everyone. You can send a reinforcing memo to praise someone and thank that person for the good job done. That someone could be a department manager in your Kansas plant or Lucy Lake, several levels removed from you.

"Do you see what a motivating effect such positive reinforcement will have on people?" asked the Infoman. "The power of this report is that it breaks down barriers of communication and helps you treat people right."

*

*The Secret To Good
Management
Is
TREATING PEOPLE RIGHT*

*Based On
GOOD INFORMATION*

*

Scott knew how true that was. His people deserved to be treated right, and information was the key. "I fully agree that One Page Management delivers good information, but we also have to provide our managers with the human skills necessary to treat people right."

"Exactly," said the Infoman. "When these three One Page Reports are produced, the preparation work will be over, but the management challenge will begin. You will have to train your managers to be interested in the success of their subordinates, to communicate, problem-solve, and catch people doing the right things. When your people begin to implement these skills, they will find that their One Page Reports are great management tools."

Scott was nodding his head all the time. He had one last question to ask the Infoman. "Who prepares the Management Report?" he inquired.

"For a company this size, the computer should be used to prepare this report," responded the Infoman. "If you use a computer, you can connect it to all your information sources, manual or automated. The computer can then funnel the data and customize the reports for your managers. You can build additional capability into the computer program to allow managers to ask for information beyond what is on their One Page Reports.

"As your managers become comfortable and begin to rely on the One Page Reports, they will become less and less dependent on the hundreds of reports I saw in your office on my first visit. Instead of distributing those reports to your managers, you may want to keep one copy filed in an information library where managers may go if they need to look up data. You may also want to stop producing many reports nobody uses."

Scott was listening attentively. The Infoman remembered Scott's earlier remarks about computers and said, "If you didn't have computers, here is how this report could be prepared manually, although it would be cumbersome.

"You would ask managers to discuss in 'team meetings' the good news and the bad news from their areas and to fill out the Management Report themselves.

"This exercise would serve as a useful management activity. By team meeting, I mean the meeting of a manager with his direct subordinates. That means each manager would attend two team meetings weekly, one as the team leader, the other as a team member. In this way the teams would be interlocked within the organization and would become the vehicle for effective communication.

"The discussion of the good news or the bad news in these meetings will be based on the team members' Feedback Reports. In the upper right-hand area of a blank report, the team leader would write at least one item each direct subordinate feels proud enough about to share with others.

"In the lower right-hand area the team leader would write one problem each direct subordinate is working on."

"How about the left-hand side of the report?" asked Scott.

"Those can be entered by the team leader based on the exception memos he has received from lower levels."

"The manual solution you've presented doesn't seem too bad," commented Scott.

"It has its merits, but I still recommend the computer solution combined with team meetings."

The Infoman turned to Scott. He smiled, and made his concluding remarks with confidence.

"Your main goal is to turn Xcorp around," he said. "I believe you can do it. I believe in you."

Scott was sad to see the Infoman preparing to leave. He had enjoyed his meetings with this mysterious person.

"Will we see you again?"

"You don't need me," said the Infoman.

"You've just gotten us going on One Page Management. You can't leave us now. What if we run into problems we can't handle?"

"Then I'll contact you," replied the Infoman as he wished Scott well in his journey to success and said good-bye.

PART IV

*The Power of
One Page Management*

ONE Page Management became the way of life at Xcorp. Managers applied the concepts to their work, and many used them in their personal lives. Their successes reinforced their desire to keep on improving.

Xcorp put One Page Management on the computer. It allowed the company to restructure the flow of information to people. The three One Page Reports were the main management reports circulating at Xcorp. They satisfied managers' primary information needs. To supplement the three One Page Reports, managers were directed to information libraries where all Xcorp reports were kept.

Managers spent the time the computer had saved them in coaching, problem-solving, and action planning.

One Monday morning, six months after One Page Reports had become a way of life at Xcorp, Scott received his Management Report.

THE MANAGEMENT REPORT FOR
BRIAN SCOTT

Week Ending December 7

	LOWER LEVELS		DIRECT SUBORDINATES					
	Names	Success Factors	Names	Success Factors	Status	Goal	Period	Trend
Positives	Arnold Turner	% Scrap	Brown	% Overall Efficiency	98.8	98	3	G
			Patrick	% Unsettled Grievances	5	10	2	G
				% Turnover	5	8	1	G
			Rayner	% Payables over 30 Days	10	5	8	B
			Clark	% Sales over Quota	12	5	1	G
	Names	Problem	Names	Success Factors	Status	Goal	Period	Trend
Negatives	Joe Davis	% Rejects	Brown	% Overall First Quality	90	94	5	B
			Patrick	% Managers Trained	5	10	3	B
				Incentive project	Late	Oct 9	10	—
			Rayner	% Accounts Receivable over 30 Days	40	20	8	B
			Clark	% Sales Priority Product	10	30	3	G

Scott was examining his Management Report when his eyes fell upon a name in the upper-left hand corner. The corner had been blank until this time.

"Arnold Turner! That sounds familiar. Who is he?" wondered Scott.

Scott called his secretary.

"Can you find out who Arnold Turner is?"

A few minutes later Joanne Evans informed Scott that Turner was the department manager in the Kansas wire plant.

"I'd like to meet Turner," said Scott. "Please arrange for him to come in one morning next week. Also inform Brown and the Kansas plant manager that I'm seeing Turner to thank him personally for keeping our scrap down."

Joanne Evans called Turner in Kansas. She congratulated him on his performance and invited him to fly to the Xcorp corporate headquarters to meet Scott. The meeting was set for Tuesday afternoon.

Turner was thrilled with the news. He deserved it. He had become the champion of One Page Management and had used its principles to help Xcorp achieve substantial savings.

Every time Turner was promoted, he had defined new Critical Success Factors and goals appropriate to his new job. Whenever he consistently met his Satisfactory Goal Levels, he had tightened them.

Today Turner's efforts were coming to fruition. He was important enough for the CEO to want to see him. He smiled, picked up the phone, and shared the good news with his wife.

During the weekend, Turner prepared for his meeting with the CEO by reading the latest reports on the performance of the Kansas plant. He also read several books and magazine articles he knew Scott had been promoting.

On Tuesday morning Turner kissed his wife good-bye and drove his car to the airport. He got on the plane, took a two-hour flight, and arrived at the impressive Xcorp headquarters around noon.

This was the first time Turner had seen the building. He felt happy, and proud of working for Xcorp. All his hard work had been worth it.

After he had lunch at a nearby restaurant, Turner walked to Scott's area. He was excited and confident. He greeted Scott's secretary.

"Please have a seat. Mr. Scott will be with you in a few minutes," said Evans.

Soon the door opened and Scott walked toward Turner with a smile and a warm welcome.

Scott had investigated the Kansas plant's performance and had discovered that Turner was the one who had helped save millions of dollars for Xcorp through improved performance, mainly scrap reduction.

"I saw your name on my Management Report," said Scott.

"I know," said Turner. "My Feedback Report indicated that the news was coming to you. But I wasn't sure you would notice it."

"Tell me," asked Scott, "how did you get to be such an excellent performer?"

"I owe it to setting clear goals, keeping track of my progress, and getting people involved in problem-solving."

Scott thought that this was a pretty good description of One Page Management. "I'm glad we implemented One Page Management," he said proudly.

Soon Scott and Turner were talking about several topics related to the company. Scott liked Turner's honesty and enthusiasm. Many points Turner was bringing up agreed with Scott's own views. Scott felt comfortable with Turner. He asked Turner if he was free to stay and attend a cocktail party that evening. Turner agreed.

Scott and Turner discussed many serious issues facing the company that evening. Turner had the grass-roots perspective and presented some creative ideas on major issues facing Xcorp. He had gained considerable experience in problem-solving while dealing with the negatives on his Feedback Report.

Scott had arranged for his own limousine to drive Turner to the airport. He saw Turner to the limousine.

Scott told Turner that he was thanking him on behalf of the shareholders of Xcorp for the superb job Turner had done in keeping the scrap down at the Kansas plant. Scott then smiled and said, "I am personally thankful because you're helping me succeed in turning Xcorp around." With those words Scott and Turner shook hands and said good-bye.

Turner was excited. He was so high he didn't need a plane to fly him home to Kansas. He had a grin on his face all the way home.

SIX months after Scott had met Turner, Xcorp was showing significant signs of recovery. Scott had made drastic cutbacks, eliminated several product lines, streamlined management, and introduced new products and services. Contrary to Scott's previous experience, the problems at Xcorp were largely organizational. Scott's business acumen, along with his responsiveness to the conditions of the company, were responsible for Xcorp's turnaround. When One Page Management became the way of life, it helped sustain the improvements. The recovery was substantial and turned into a boom.

The improved quality of Xcorp products boosted sales, while productivity increased. The result was a substantial increase in Xcorp's net margin. The shareholders and the Board of Directors were happy.

On the second anniversary of his term with Xcorp, Scott reflected back on his first visit with the Infoman. He could now see why the Infoman was so excited about One Page Management. This system had helped Scott introduce change in the company. It was not like many good ideas that come and go without having any real or lasting effect.

One Page Management was a system that covered the organization from the top to the grass roots. It allowed change to take effect because it was rooted in managers' aspirations for excellence, and in corporate information. Because the system promoted fairness and communicated accurate information, managers' old habits gave way to new ones that conformed with this system. Scott recalled the Infoman's analogy with the sea of information. He was pleased that One Page Management was both an agent of change and the system that saved managers from drowning.

Scott remembered how he had defined success as turning Xcorp around. Now it had happened in just two years. He was pleased. He wanted to thank the Infoman. He knew what the Infoman would ask in return for all the benefits Xcorp was realizing from One Page Management:

*

*Share
One Page Management
With
Others*

*

Concept Praisings

We would like to acknowledge the contributions of the following people during the development and implementation of the concepts incorporated in this book.

Jim Dewberry, Buddy Roberts, Bob Bishop, and **Dwight Carlisle** for nurturing the ideas of One Page Management during the early stages.

Ken Blanchard, Larry Miller, and **Aubrey Daniels** for teaching us many things about performance management.

Russ Harrison for his constant encouragement to apply the concepts to project environments.

Bob Guyton, Joe Anderer, Bill Garwood, Mike Piazza, Harry Holliman, Bob Rutland, Guy Rutland, John Singleton, Tom Cook, Bill Capps, Fred Cisweski, Frank McCreary, Craig Clonts, Abbott Whitney, Peggie Chappelle, and **Mary Ann Keeney** for promoting One Page Management in their organizations.

Personal Praisings

We would like to acknowledge the invaluable contributions made by the following people in bringing this book into being.

Linda Khadem for being our main consultant during every stage of this book.

Ken Blanchard for being our mentor and friend, for making many valuable suggestions throughout the entire process, and for giving us One Minute Praisings along the way.

Pat Zigarmi for critically editing the manuscript in the final stages.

Margaret McBride for being our literary agent, friend, and constant support.

The staff of William Morrow and Company, Inc., and particularly **Al Marchioni** and **Pat Golbitz** for believing in us and for becoming excited enough about the concepts of One Page Management to publish and distribute this book.

Kelsey Tyson and **Marjorie Blanchard** for their encouragement, constructive feedback, and support.

Ramin Khadem for editing the manuscript from the financial viewpoint.

Riaz Khadem would also like to thank:

Rex Pulford, my technical consultant and friend for his invaluable work on the technical development of the One Page Management System.

Doug Ruhe and **Bill Geisseler** for believing in my information solution.

John Montgomery for encouraging me during a difficult period of my career.

Peggy Hunt for being a loyal and talented secretary from start to finish of this manuscript.

A special thanks to my parents from whom I have never ceased to learn, to my brothers and sisters for their encouragement, and to my children, **Nasr, Tina,** and **Gregory,** for all the weekends they gave up.

Bob Lorber would like to thank:

Gordon Anderson, Bud Ogden, Ethan Jackson, Brady Justice, Alan McMillen, Gary Anderson, George Argyros, Ray Watt, Ken Ramsey, and **Jim Morrell.**

My partners, **Kef Kamai** and **Donna Sillman,** and the fine staff of Lorber Kamai Associates, Inc.

My executive assistant, **Muriel Swartz,** for the constant attention to detail and excellence.

My wife, **Sandy,** and my two daughters, **Tracie** and **Lindie.**

About the Authors

Dr. Riaz Khadem, a leading expert in the role of information in productivity improvement and culture change, is president of INFOTRAC, INC., a company specializing in customized information systems, headquartered in Atlanta, Georgia.

Dr. Khadem received a bachelor's degree in engineering from the University of Illinois, a master's degree in engineering science from Harvard, and a Doctorate in mathematics from Oxford University (Balliol College). His publications include *Information Retrieval of Large Data Bases, How to Approach Office Automation, Having Your Reports and Using Them Too,* and *The One Page Report—Tool for Managers.*

After his university education, Khadem pursued an academic career as lecturer, research associate, and assistant professor of mathematics at the University of Southampton, Northwestern University, and Université Laval, where he became associate professor before leaving academia to apply his education to the practical problems of organizations.

Khadem has implemented One Page Management Systems for a number of corporations in manufacturing, transportation, textile, and agribusiness.

Dr. Robert Lorber, an internationally known expert in performance improvement, high performance teams, and corporate culture, is president of Lorber Kamai Associates, Inc., a company specializing in the strategic design and implementation of productivity improvement systems, headquartered in Orange and Los Angeles, California.

Dr. Lorber received his BA and MA degrees from the University of California at Davis and in 1974 was awarded a Ph.D. in applied behavioral science and organizational psychology. His publications include *Effective Feedback: The Key to Engineering Performance, Managing Data vs. Gut Feeling, How to Implement Change: Supervise and Lead.* His publication *Putting the One Minute Manager to Work,* co-authored with Dr. Kenneth H. Blanchard, was on *The New York Times* best-seller list.

Dr. Lorber and his organization have implemented productivity systems for small, medium, and *Fortune* 500 companies throughout the United States as well as the Middle East, South America, Mexico, Africa, Europe, and Canada.

Services Available

The following services are available to help organizations implement One Page Management:

- Consulting to guide clients through the implementation of One Page Management

- Seminars and workshops from one to five days to help managers develop and apply the principles of One Page Management

- Software system (TOPS) to produce the three One Page Reports

For further information about One Page Management contact:

INFOTRAC, INC.
600 River Valley Road, Suite B
Atlanta, Georgia 30328

404-843-2589